The Anger From Within

By Keith Mitchell

The Anger From Within
A true story of one man's battle with the grips of addiction
by Keith Mitchell

Printed in the United States of America

ISBN 9781613798720

Unless otherwise indicated, Bible quotations are taken from The New Scofiel Study Bible. Copyright © 1984 by Oxford University Press, New York.

www.xulonpress.com

DEDICATION

I would like to dedicate this book to the memory of my beautiful mother and my younger brother, Greg. You both meant so much to me during your time here on this earth. I love you both.

ACKNOWLEDGEMENTS

I would like to thank first, My Lord and Savior, Jesus Christ for never leaving my side and being with me through all of the obstacles that I have endured in my life. And also allowing me to have this time to share with you this story and how He loves all of His children and how He will so desperately go to any length to reach us, so that we can share an eternity of being with Him.

To my beautiful Wife, Leanne: Thank you for loving me and being by my side through so many tough times. Thank you for being an incredible mother to our beautiful children Kade and Mary-Micah.

To my Daughters, Lindsey and Logann: Words will never express how much I love each one of you. You are both so beautiful and I am so proud of you. Although you have both grown into beautiful young women, you will always be your daddy's little girls.

To My Dad and Step mother, Lefty and Kathy Mitchell: I love you both and I thank you for all of your support through the years. Dad, you have always been my hero and you will continue to be forever. Thanks Dad, I Love you!

To my In-laws, Johnny and Rebecca McDaniel's and Tommy and Liz Lord: I know that there have been so many trying times during my marriage to your daughter. Thank you for your patience. I love you all.

To the Minister's of Teen Challenge, Brother Greg, Brother Stanley, Brother Gary, and Brother Sampson: I can never truly express the love that I have in my heart for all of you. Not only for me, but I know that I speak on behalf of all of the men and women that have ever come through the Louisiana Teen Challenge program, and now have a better and more productive life because you took the time with each one of us, one on one, and shared the Gospel of Jesus Christ with us.

To my Pastor at Turning Point Church, Jeff Wickwire: Thank you for preaching the truth. I know without a shadow of a doubt that the Lord led me and my family to Turning Point Church. The Church that I love and I now call home.

To my friends, Keith and Kayla Johnson: Thank you for your diligence in your prayers when I would call late at night and say that I was struggling and you were always faithful in your prayers and you have always been there for me.

Sandy Batterton: I will never forget being in the ICU suffering from an overdose and you were my nurse. You wept, cried, and prayed for me. I have never forgotten that or you. I love you and God Bless!

To my childhood friends: Tom and David Bowman, Taz and Todd Ellett, Rob McClellan, Steve Scot, Steven Gilbert, Gary Rambin, Ross Atkins, Stuart Fortner, and many others that reached out to me in High School and invited me to Bible studies and were always concerned for me.

Tony Stelly, Russ Thompson and Scot Brasuell: Thank you for the many hours you spent with me when I was at my lowest, talking and praying with me and for me.

I would also like to thank Matthew Powell, Brother Bo Nicholson, Lorissa Owens, Kyle and Jill Williams, K.D. and Karen Williams, Brad and Trisha Martin, Priscilla Bowman, Al and Barbara Brasuell, Carter Lewis, Todd Carter Tony Farley, Chuck and Debbie Barham, Steven Kaled, Haley Brown, Revette Richard, Shea Rhinehart, Chad and Nichole Johnson, I love you too!

I would like to say a special thank you to Carolyn Smith and Julie Graham. When you saw me veering from the path of righteousness, you had the courage out of love to call me and tell me so. And I thank you for that.

And thanks to anyone else who has ever poured into me or prayed for me. I love you and God Bless!

TABLE OF CONTENTS

INTRODUCTION

IT IS FINISHED

My Drug addiction spanned for over 20 years of my life. It was an addiction that controlled my mind and every thought. I was a hard core user. I could never get high enough or be high enough. I always wanted more. My drugs of choice were cocaine and heroin. I also used many of other drugs. My hope in writing this book is to show how powerful the Lord Jesus Christ is. And to show how much He loves each and every one of us. Our God granted salvation to all, He shows no favoritism. He loves the rich and the poor, the strong and the weak, and the lost and the found. Even the drug addict, the alcoholic, and the prostitute.

Many of the people from my hometown, in Ruston, Louisiana, thought that my addiction would kill me. And to be quite honest, I did too. It would take too long to list all the insanity that went along with my drug addiction, but you will read enough to see why I knew I was going to die using drugs. I have never written a book before. The only reason I have written this one is because I was led of the Holy Spirit. I hope people will read this book for a couple of reasons. First, it will show the awesome saving power of Jesus Christ. And secondly, I know that it will give insight on the perspec-

tive of someone who lived a life of torment here on earth...
But you see, the Lord had a different plan for my life:

Jeremiah 29:11
*For I know the plans I have for you declares the Lord,
plans to prosper you and not to harm you, plans to give
you hope and a future.*

My Name is Keith Mitchell and this is my story.

MY CHILDHOOD

M y Childhood was really great. It was just me and my little brother along with my parents. I had cousins that we were close to, but they all lived in other cities and states. My parents didn't make a lot of money and we weren't rich at all. My dad was a blue collar guy who worked really hard for his money to support our family. He has always been very well liked and respected in my hometown. He was pretty much a loner. He had lots of friends, but he always would just spend his time with our family.

My dad was the epitome of the family guy. He taught Greg and I not to steal. We were always taught to respect grownups, and to never start a fight, but at the same time, not let anyone run over us. I can even remember when we were like four and five years old we couldn't wait for my dad to come home from work. He was a linesman. He climbed telephone poles for a living. He would build power lines that would sometimes run through the Louisiana swamps. I can remember my mom would ask him how his day went and he would say that he was working in the swamps so he had to eat his lunch sitting on the top of a telephone pole between two cross arms, and that his co-workers would run his lunch box up a hand line to him.

My mom would give him enough money to buy a candy bar and a coke, and every day when his co-workers would drop him off at the end of our street, Greg and I would be sitting in the front yard, out close to the street, waiting to see our dad, the man that we idolized. Once we would see him, we would jump to our feet and shout to our mom that we could see him walking down the street. She would say, "Okay, you can go to him, but watch out for cars."

Dad would be toting his linesman belt over his shoulder and he would have his climbing gaffs in one hand and his lunch box in the other. He always wore his hard hat the same way, kind of tilted back on his head. We would run up the street to meet him. When we were about 15 yards in front of him, he would kneel down, set all of his gear down and open up his arms for his two boys to get to him. Once we got there, he would hug us, kiss us and tell us how much he missed us. He never failed to grab his lunch box and he would say, "Alright boys, who wants to carry my lunch box home?" We would both reach for it and he would say, "Okay, but you guys better check out what's inside first."

It never failed. We would open his lunch box and there would be two candy bars in it. Our eyes would light up every day because we knew that our dad had a surprise waiting for us. He never failed us. It wasn't until years later that our mom would tell us that dad never bought a coke or a candy bar for himself.

When I was in grade school, I can remember being so scared that dad would have an accident at work, either get electrocuted or would fall off of a telephone pole. I can remember hearing an ambulance when I would be sitting in class and I would almost start crying at the thought of something happening to my pop. We were his pride and joy. Every second he was home he would spend with us wrestling and playing. He taught us how to play ball and how to ride our bikes, but I think the greatest thing that dad ever did for us was to teach us how to hunt and fish.

On weekends, he and my papaw would take us riding in the country to look for places to deer hunt. We would stop by the local convenience store called Goolsbys and by a honey bun and chocolate milk. That was the same store in town that we would by our fishing baits when he would take us fishing. We would always see some of our schoolmates with their dads buying bait as they too were getting ready to go on a big fishing trip with their dads. It always made us feel special that our dad was taking us because we knew that once back at school, we would talk to those same kids about how many fish we had caught. Once we got down to the hunting woods, he would let me and Greg sit in the back of the truck on the fender wells and look for deer tracks on the dirt roads that we were driving on. We would see lots of deer and would often fight over who saw the most deer tracks.

Me and Greg

As we grew older, Greg and I would spend so many fall afternoons together behind our house on the creek banks squirrel hunting and duck hunting, laughing, hunting and trying to outhunt one another. Both of us were really competitive and that just made it all the more exciting. To this day, I think that is why we both wound up being really good hunters. I do remember this one time when we first moved down to the country, Greg must have been 13 and I was 14, our closest neighbor was Mrs. Robinson, she was a sweet old lady and she lived about a quarter of a mile down the road past our house. There was a bridge on the road about 100 yards past her house. That is where Greg and I would meet up when we were hunting.

Well, on this day, I was directly behind our house and Greg had walked down the road all the way to the bridge at Mrs. Robinson's house. He had gone into the woods and begun hunting. The later it got, the more he shot. All of a sudden, it sounded like world war III had just begun. I remember thinking, *What in the world?* Then, the shooting stopped. About 10 minutes later, I heard something coming through the woods. It sounded like a tornado. I was sitting beside a tree with my shotgun between my legs when I saw Greg coming. His pace was fast and furious. He never saw me.

Once he was about 15 yards in front of me, I yelled, "HEY! WHERE ARE YOU GOING?" I thought it would scare him. It didn't faze him.

He said, "Keith, you gotta come help me!"

I said, "What's wrong?"

He explained, "Man, I have got ducks down everywhere at the bridge."

I said, "Really."

He replied, "Man, it was awesome."

I asked, "Are there any more coming in?"

He answered, "I don't know, probably. C'mon, let's go, hurry up."

We took off to the bridge. Once we got down close to the bridge, we came to a big part of the creek where it kind of opened up with a lot of water. It looked sort of like a pond. I stood there looking out across the water with a look of horror on my face. Greg looked at me with this big old grin on his face and said, "What cha think?"

I replied, "YOU IDIOT! We are so dead."

He asked, "What do you mean?"

I said, "Greg, you have killed all of Mrs. Robinson's tamed ducks."

He said, "Huh?"

I answered, "Dad's going to kill us!"

Sure enough, before we even made it back to the house, Mrs. Robinson had called Dad. He waited until supper to ask us how our hunt went. We were both really quiet. We avoided eye contact. And finally, he just asked us if there was anything we wanted to tell him. Greg looked at me first. I just put my head down and started to tell him the truth. As I started to speak, Greg blurted out, "Dad, I shot Mrs. Robinson's ducks."

Greg started crying and I knew he was afraid he was getting ready to get the beating of his life. I felt sorry for him so I said, "Dad, I shot um, too. It was both of our faults."

Greg looked at me in shock. I figured it would be easier if we both took the heat. We were always afraid that dad was going to give us the beating of our lives, but he never did. Now, don't get me wrong, he had this vein that would poke out on the side of his head around the temple area. When that vein would pop out on his head, we knew to steer clear of Dad. That day on the creek was not the only time Greg got me in trouble.

On another occasion we were behind the house hunting. We were walking down the creek bank together when Greg said, "Keith! What is that?"

I looked up, and there hanging in a tree was a huge beehive. I said, "Greg, that is a Beehive."

He replied, "Man, that thing is huge."

I said, "C'mon, let's go!"

Before I could even start to take a step, I heard Greg's gun go off. I looked up and there was a black cloud that had formed instantly just right out in front of us.

I screamed, "ARE YOU CRAZY?" I said, "Jump in the creek." I dropped my shot gun and grabbed him and jumped into the creek. We got popped a couple of times on the head. Every time we came up for a breath, they would be hovering right above us. We would stay under as long as we could. Finally, they settled down and we were able to get out of the creek.

I said, "Are you nuts?"

He said, "Keith!"

I answered, "What?"

He replied, "My 12 gauge is in the creek."

I said, "You jumped in with it, didn't you?"

He gave me that crooked smile and nodded his head. I said, "You're killing me Greg."

There are so many more memories that I have that will last me my entire lifetime.

Greg, from the time he was very little, wet the bed. He would try really hard not to. My mom would have to wash his sheets every night and she grew tired of having to wash so many loads of clothes every day. He had a small bladder and he would sleep so hard that he just would never wake up. Finally, one day she said that the next time that he wet the bed she was going to hang his sheets on the clothes line where everyone on our school bus would see them. Well, looking back now that I'm grown, I know that she would have never done that and it was just a scare tactic. Well, it worked because every night I would listen for him to wet the bed. We shared a bedroom together. I don't know how much of it was that I felt really sorry for him, or maybe that I would be embarrassed for the both of us, but I would listen and the moment that I would hear him start to wet the bed, I would shout at him and wake him up. Sometimes, I would just make him get up at least twice a night, and that worked out pretty good. On those nights that I would just be exhausted from the night before, I would wake up to find his bed wet and I would wake him up and we would strip his bed. Luckily, the washer and dryer were on our end of the house. Then, I would have to stay up and wait to put his sheets in the dryer. I would make him get in the bed with me until right before it was time for Mom and Dad to get up. We would go into stealth mode so that the whole transaction would run smoothly. Greg did tell me lots of times that he loved me for doing this for him and so it was worth all those sleepless nights, and knowing that it would keep him from a severe whipping and being embarrassed by a school bus full of kids.

We got older, started high school and Dad eventually moved us back to Ruston. That is where we wanted to be because that's where all of our childhood friends were. Personally, when I got my driver's license, the last place I wanted to be was stuck out in the country. I loved living in the country for the hunting, but once I became a freshman in high school, things changed. I wanted to play football. The school that I was going to didn't have a football team. Once I got to Ruston High School, I would get kicked off the team every time I went out. Somebody would hit me and I would try and fight them right there. The coaches told me that I should join a boxing club, and so I did. Once we moved to Ruston, my parents found a house and once again we had to share another bedroom. I remember I was embarrassed by that for several years.

I would never invite my buddies over to spend the night because they would have found out that Greg and I shared a bedroom together. Looking back now, that was the greatest thing that could have ever happened to us. We spent so many nights lying in our beds talking about football and baseball.

Greg loved basketball and he loved Dr J. We would sometimes stay up all night talking about deer hunting, squirrel
hunting and where we wanted to build deer stands for the
next year. We went over, in our heads, a thousand times what
kind of houses we wanted when we got married. Greg always
said he wanted a Log Cabin and he would have a big pond in
his back yard stocked with largemouth bass. I wanted a Log
cabin, as well. We both said that we would build on opposite
sides of Mom and Dad's house. We would tease each other
about what our kids were going to look like. He said my kids
would have a big nose like me, and I would tell him that his
kids would be born with jagged teeth.

When he was 13, a kid that lived down the street threw
a rock at him and broke his front tooth in half. My mom
took him, at least a half dozen times, to the dentist to get it
fixed, but he would just knock it right back out again. And
so, he picked at me about my nose and I gave him the business about his tooth. Me and some of my buddies would tell
him that his mouth looked like the lake D'arbonne stump
field. That's a local lake that we used to fish on. It had a
ton of broken trees sticking up out of the water and they
were nothing more than a bunch of old stumps. He would
get fighting mad.

There was this one time when we were with some of our
buddies in Jr. High School. We went down to the railroad
tracks and the train came by. The train was carrying a load of
brand new cars and trucks. One of the boys picked up a rock
and threw it at a car. We all stood there looking at each other
for a minute and, all of a sudden, everyone was picking up
rocks and throwing them at the cars. I think that is one of the
only times in my life that I had better sense. Greg picked up
a rock and started to throw it and I grabbed his hand and I
said to him, "Dad will kill us."

He dropped the rock. Sure enough, somehow, the Police
found us. The guys that we were with were good friends and

kept us from a beating. They told the police that we hadn't thrown a rock and kept my dad from having to pay for all of the damage that the other dads had to shell out. Greg and I loved people and loved to have a good time. We were both very rowdy in school. We, neither one of us, were model students in school. I remember, on several occasions, both of us being called to the principal's office at the same time for different reasons. He would get in trouble for dipping snuff at school, and I would get in a fight or would get caught skipping class. The funny thing is we were rough boys. We fought just like all brothers do. We had some knock downs, too. I was older and for sure had the worst temper. I could whip him, but I wasn't going to let anyone else whip him. Not if I was around. Greg and I were as close as two brothers could be. We shared so many laughs and made so many memories when we were kids. Whether it was building forts in the woods with our buddies or building bicycle ramps and breaking a bone or two, we were always together and we were always having the best time we could possibly have. He was my baby brother and I loved him dearly.

I first used Cocaine in June of 1982. I remember it well. I remember it because that was the month that my little brother, my best friend and only sibling passed away. Greg, my baby brother, was killed on a motorcycle that had been a gift from my mom and dad after high school graduation. When Greg died, to say it was devastating would be an understatement. My family fell apart. My dad completely shut himself out from everyone. I remember he couldn't talk about Greg for years. My dad really loved us boys. Looking back, now that I have my own children, I can't even imagine what he and my mother went through. I remember my mom having to be sedated at the hospital when Greg died. It took years for things to get back to even a shade of normalcy.

Greg and I were especially close. After my Jr. High years in school, my dad moved us to the country. And so, all we had was each other to play with. Looking back, those were the best years of my life. There is an innocence, when you are a kid, that doesn't last very long. Greg was a wonderful kid. He loved life and spent every second of it smiling. I can remember when we were kids in the heat of summer playing baseball, a cloud would come up and it would become one of those quick thunderstorms that would only last a few minutes. And as soon as it would pass, you could see the steam rising up off of the asphalt. Greg and I would run over and stand in the middle of the road and he would say, "Don't cha love the smell of the rain on the hot road." We would laugh and go back to playing ball. I can still remember the way that the leather smelled from my baseball glove.

I went hunting and fishing with Greg, my dad and grandfather. We chased lightning bugs and put them in jars, just like every kid who lives in the south has done. We had a great childhood. I'm telling you these things to paint a picture of what my childhood was like, because in the upcoming chapters you will see how the devil used my little brother's death to take me on a ride that took me further than I wanted to go and kept me longer than I wanted to stay.

I know there are people out there that think drug addicts are just horrible people who have no purpose in life. Some people will say they are the scum of the earth, or they are just sorry, horrible, pathetic, Loser's. Well, please remember that at one time they were probably a normal everyday person, but because of something, very traumatic, that happened in their lives, they felt the deep pain of losing a family member, the loss of their job, or the rejection of not being able to fit in at school. There are many reasons people take drugs just to cope in this thing we call life. I know that for people who have never experienced the grips of addiction, it's hard to understand what I am talking about, but let me give you an example of what I'm talking about.

There were times in my addiction that even the thought of running out of cocaine would put me in a state of panic. When I would call my dealer and he would not answer the phone, I would go crazy screaming like a mad person, cursing him and calling him every name in the book. When he did finally answer, he'd say that he had the drugs and for me to come over and pick them up. On the ride over to his house, my stomach would begin to cramp and I would lose control of my bowels. I had to get to his house. In a state of panic, I would get there, run in and pay him, and, with shaking hands, tear open the baggie and take the dope! Within a few minutes, I would settle back down and drive back to my home with my drugs. Then about six hours later, the same episode would begin all over again. It's an insane madness.

THE WRECK

I can still remember the day Greg died like it was yesterday. It happened on Monday June 7th at about noon. Greg was working a summer job helping a local contractor build an apartment complex. He was on his way home for lunch to eat with my Mom and Dad, as he always did on his lunch break. My Dad and Greg would sit at the bar in my parent's kitchen and eat lunch every day. My Mom at about 12:15 said to my Dad, "I wonder where Greg is at. He is usually always here by now."

My dad replied, "He will be here in a few minutes."

A few minutes later, they heard someone come to the door. A buddy of mine and Greg's burst through the door and yelled to my dad, "Mr. Mitchell, Greg has been in a wreck up in front of Trinity Church."

My dad asked our friend how bad it was and if Greg was ok? The friend said, "Mr. Mitchell, I think it's pretty bad."

My mom started crying. They jumped in my mom's car and drove to the scene of the accident. When they pulled up, the ambulance was just getting there as well. My dad told my mom to stay in the car. He looked at her and said, "Rose, stay here. I don't know how bad it is. I want you to stay here."

She never got out of the car. I've always been glad that she never got out of that vehicle. Dad ran up to the accident and there was, already, a bunch of people gathered around.

Ruston is a small town and everyone pretty much knows each other. The Police in town all knew my dad because he, too, worked for the City of Ruston. They ran up to him and tried to keep him from seeing Greg in the condition that he was in.

They said, "Lefty, you don't need to see Greg like this."

My dad wouldn't have any part of it. He said to them, "That's my baby lying there and I want to see him."

They let him approach Greg. I wished he wouldn't have seen him in that condition. I guess any man would react the same way. They loaded Greg into the ambulance and drove him to the hospital.

I wasn't living at home anymore. I was going to college and working part time. I was working for a T.V. cable company installing cable. I was at work when a call came over the radio and my office told me to go to the hospital because my little brother had been in a motorcycle accident. I drove over to the hospital, to the emergency room, and there were a lot of folks starting to gather outside of the hospital. Mostly, kids from the high school in town. I rushed inside. As the doors opened, time went into slow motion. I remember looking to my left and seeing my fiancé, her roommate, and some other friends sitting in the waiting room. They were all crying. There were all these people in there. I remember thinking, *What are all these people doing here? And how long ago did this happen?* I saw my mom with a bunch of people that I knew and they were all trying to comfort her. There was a nurse giving her a shot to sedate her. She was hysterical. We had never been through anything like this before. We were such a close family and this seemed to be like a really bad dream.

I looked down the hallway and saw my grandfather running toward me. I said, "Papaw, where is dad?"

He answered, "He is back at the operating room. You need to go back there with him."

I started running and over the intercom I heard them call out a code blue. I started shaking all over my body. I went through the doors and saw my dad standing there with his head down. He was standing right outside the doors of the operating room. I walked up to him and he looked at me and said, "He isn't going to make it."

I said, "What?"

He said, "Our little buddy's not going to make it."

I replied, "Dad, you don't know that."

He stared into my eyes and said, "Son, I saw his little body lying there." He began to cry. He continued, "Our little buddy is all messed up."

I grabbed my dad and hugged him. I said, "Dad, you don't know that."

We stood there for a while and my dad had gotten very quite. A few minutes later, a nurse that I knew came out of the operating room and I stopped her. I said, "Renee, how is he?"

She looked at us both and said, "Keith, I'm not going to lie. He is in really bad shape. But, there is a chance that he will pull through."

That is what I wanted to hear. I looked at Dad and said, "See Dad, there is hope. I'm going to check on Mom."

He said, "Okay." He said he was going to stay there.

I walked back down to the front of the building. I remembered thinking about what my dad had said about how badly Greg's body was. He has never mentioned it since. I knew for him to say that, it must have been really bad. As I got to the front of the emergency room, there were people everywhere. I walked into the room where my mom was lying down and there were a bunch of ladies in there with her. I don't know why I didn't tell her what the nurse had told me and dad. I guess I realized that she had calmed down and she was just lying there quietly with these ladies holding her hands. I walked up to her and kissed her on the cheek.

One of the grownups standing by the door said, "Keith, a couple of your buddies are standing out here wanting to talk to you."

I walked out into the hallway and there stood two of my best buddies. They said, "Hey man, how's "Little Mitch" doing?"

Greg and I were in school together for years because we're only a year and a half apart. And when any one would mention our names, they would always refer to us as "Big Mitch" or "Little Mitch." I think we both really liked the references. I know that I did.

I said to my buddies, "Hey guys, my jeep is parked out in front of the emergency room. Let's go and move it right quick because I need to go and check on Greg and see how my dad is holding up."

We walked outside and moved the jeep. I remember looking out into the parking lot and I don't know for sure how many kids were out in the parking lot, but it was a whole bunch. That has always stood out in the back of my mind at how much Greg was loved in our home town. As we stepped out of the Jeep, the director of nursing at the hospital, that I knew really well, was walking up to me. The reason I knew her is because her daughter and Greg where in the same grade and she was Greg's first crush. As Mrs. Martin walked up, I could tell something wasn't right. I could see by the look in her eyes that she was about to give me some bad news.

She said, "Keith, I'm so sorry. Greg is gone sweetie."

I said, "What? You don't know what you're talking about. I just spoke to a nurse fifteen minutes ago and she said that there was hope."

She hugged my neck and I felt every drop of blood in my body rush to my brain. I just felt like it was a really bad nightmare that I couldn't wake up from. My buddies, Scot and Tim, started crying and hugged me. I remember telling them that I had to get to my dad. I ran back into the hospital and was met by my Papaw once again. He said with quivering lips, "Boy! I can't go in there and get your daddy. You're going to have to go in there and get him."

I asked, "Where is he?"

He replied, "He is in there with your baby brother."

I remember asking Papaw to check on my mom and I took off towards the operating room. I had never been through anything like this in my life. I just wanted to crawl under something and cry and be left alone. I knew that I was about to go someplace that I didn't want to go. I reached the doors to the O.R. and stood there a second before I went in. I didn't know how I was going to be able to take this. I opened the doors and Dad was standing there at the bed holding Greg in his arms cradled like a baby. He was talking to him just like he would any other time. I remember him telling Greg how sorry he was that he couldn't help him this time, and how much he loved him. I stood behind him wanting to explode. I couldn't believe that this was happening. I stood there while dad laid him back down on the table and watched as dad closed his eyes. I remember looking down at Greg and thinking, at that very second, how all of our plans would never come true now. I had never felt anything like this before. I was in a complete state of shock.

I finally laid my hands on my dad's back and said, "Pop, we should go check on mom now."

He turned, realized I was there, and he broke down. I was hurting so bad on the inside. I was hurting for Mom and Dad. I was hurting for Greg. I had all these emotions going on inside. I was only nineteen years old; I was still a kid myself.

My dad said, "I can't believe our little man is gone."

This can't be real. It's just a dream. As we got to the doors of the operating room, he stopped me and said, "Son, I know you don't understand this because you don't have children now. One of these days, you probably will and I hope you never ever have to feel this pain that I am feeling right now."

Now that I have my own children, I can't even imagine what they felt. As we were getting ready to leave the hospital, one of the nurses approached me and told me that I could have Greg's belongings. She said that they had to cut his clothes off of him, but he had some things in his pockets. She handed me a bag and inside the bag was his wallet, his keys and then I saw something that completely broke me down. There was a can of skoal tobacco that I had given him the night before. I was over at my mom and dad's and we had gotten into an argument over a pair of blue jeans. He had on a pair of my new jeans. And I chewed him out over it. It was something that would weigh on my heart for many years to come.

As I was leaving their house, I got in my jeep and felt really bad for the way I treated him over a pair of stinking blue jeans, so I got back out of the jeep and walked back in the house. He was sitting on the floor watching TV and I walked up behind him and popped him on the head. I said, "Hey man, I'm sorry that I acted that way over those jeans."

He looked up at me and replied, "Hey man, we are brothers. We don't need to act like that."

I said, "I'm sorry."

He stood up and we hugged each other's necks. He followed me out to my jeep. I said, "Alright bro, I will see you later."

I started backing out of the driveway and he said, "Hey Keith, hang on a second." I stopped and he continued, "Hey man, can I have a dip?"

I pulled my can out of my pocket and tossed it to him. He took a dip out of the can and then slid the can into his own pocket. I asked, "Hey man, what are you doing?"

He said, "Come on brother, let me have this can. You are going by a store on your way to your house. You can get another can."

I laughed and said, "Man, you are killing me."

He stood there and watched me back out of the driveway. That was the last time I ever spoke to my little brother. And so, when I looked into the bag and saw that can, it broke my heart. The can had a little tiny dent on the top of the lid. For years, the fact that I had fought with him the night before he died weighed heavily on me. I would think what a bad brother I had been. It seemed like I would remember all of the fights we had. And I would want to take back all of the times that we had fought. But I couldn't. I just wanted to talk to him, and tell him how much I loved him. We left the hospital and my dad walked up to me and asked me if I was alright to drive.

Before I could respond, my buddy Scot said, "Mitch, I'll drive you."

My dad stated, "We are going over to Papaw's house. I'll see you over there." He started to walk off. Then he turned around and walked over to me. He said, "I love you, Son."

I responded, "I love you too, Dad.

Scot drove us over to my mom and dad's house because I wanted to put Greg's things that the nurse had given me, up at dad's house. When we walked into their house, it felt completely different. I walked through the kitchen and I saw something that completely stopped me in my tracks. It was Greg's uneaten lunch. I stood there and all of the hurt came rushing back on me all over again. It would be the first of many moments that would stop me in my tracks.

The funeral was tough. And the next couple of weeks were even tougher. My dad completely shut everyone out. He would hardly speak. My mom was a wreck without having Greg around. He was always so loving and kind. He was a genuinely good person who had a heart of gold.

One night, I was asleep in my bed. I suppose I was having a dream. I don't know if it was a dream or not. I'll let you be the judge. I was asleep and all of a sudden, it was like the brightest light I had ever seen flashed into my bedroom. I turned to my left and there was Greg. His face was so bright. It was the only thing I could see. There was no body just his face. He said, "Hey Keith, I had a wreck didn't I?"

I answered, "Yeah, Greg, you did."

He said, "I know Mom and Dad are taking this really hard, aren't they?"

I replied, "Yeah Buddy, they are taking it really hard."

He said, "You need to stay really close to them right now and reassure them that I loved them more than anything in the world. You need to tell them that they were the best parents in the world. And Keith, you were the best brother in the world, too."

I said, "Just stay here and I'll tell them for you, Greg."

He said, "I can't do that, just please tell them that I'm okay and that I'm in a really awesome place now. I love you Keith!" And just like that, he was gone.

When I woke up in the morning, the dream was just as fresh in my mind as it is right now. I was relieved, but still very sad. My mom had just gone back to work and she was working as a secretary at a super market in town. I rushed over to tell her about the dream. When I got there, she had a huge smile on her face that kind of caught me off guard because I hadn't seen her smile in weeks. I rushed into her office and said, "Mom, you gotta hear this." I started telling her about my dream that I had last night and she started crying really hard. I said, "Mom, I'm sorry. I just thought you would be happy."

She smiled and said, "Honey, I am happy. I had a dream last night, too. In my dream, I was here in my office and the phone rang. When I answered, an operator came on the line and said I have a long distance phone call from heaven will you accept the charges. It was Greg on the other line and he told me the same exact things that he had told you in your dream."

We both sat there and cried a good while, but it was a good cry. I think that we were taking Greg's death so hard that the Lord allowed Greg to come to us in a dream to let us know that he was with the Lord and he was okay. The Bible says that the Lord will not put more on you than what you can bear.

THE ANGER FROM WITHIN

The anger, I held from within the very core of my soul, I think, started when Greg passed away. I was angry at him I guess for leaving us like he did. I was angry at myself for not wrecking his bike the day before he died, but the person I was angry with the most was God. How could you let this happen, God? Not now! He was a great kid. I was the troubled kid. I was the one who was selfish. I was the one who manipulated everyone. Greg never hurt anyone and was loved by everybody. He was the kid who would, on some weekends, stay at home with mom and dad and watch a movie, just hang out with the folks. I thought something was wrong with him. Little did I know that God knew He was going to be calling my little brother home in just a short time.

You know, we think we are so smart; we sometimes judge God and all along we never stop to think that our Lord and Savior has our best interest at heart. You know, looking back now, I understand that our God, who just so happened to love my little brother more than I could ever love him, may have had a reason for allowing Greg to leave this earth when he did. You see, what we didn't realize at the time is that if Greg would have lived, he may have been diagnosed with some horrible disease the next week and suffered a long and tragic death. I don't know that for a fact, but I will say this, it's not for me to question God in what happens in this short time here on this earth either.

God loves each and every one of us unconditionally. I do know that the Bible says that all things work for good for those whose hope is in Christ Jesus. But, to get back to my anger problems, I Hated God, I hated everyone for a long time. I hated the fact that I was on drugs and couldn't stop. I tried so hard to stop, but couldn't.

I got married when I was in college. I was 20 at the time. I was entirely too young to be married, and Greg had been dead for a year. I had already started my drug use with cocaine. My new wife was a great girl. She finished college and put her degree to use. I stopped going to school and started to work in the oil field working on a pipeline. After another year of marriage, my drug use increased and we ended the marriage. What happened next was an overdose that sent me to the hospital for the first of many trips. I was single again; I was using daily; and all I wanted to do was party around a bunch of people to forget all my troubles.

One night, there was a huge party at this girl's house in Ruston. There were at least 75 to 100 people there and I was with a couple of my friends. We had been using all day. I was high on cocaine and ecstasy. I knew the girl who was throwing the party really well, and her parents were out of town. I pretty much knew everyone that was at the party. We went into the bath room and closed the door. There was about 5 or 6 guys in the bathroom and we started going through her parent's medicine cabinet. We found all kinds of pain pills, so we broke them open and crushed some to snort them. I don't even know what all we snorted; I just did them to be doing them. Then, one of my friends said, "Mitch, open your mouth and close your eyes," and he dropped a hit of acid on my tongue. I said, "What's that?" and he told me what it was. We exited the bath room a little while later and went outside. My friend came back a few minutes later and gave me another hit of acid. Not knowing what all we had just snorted, combining cocaine, ecstasy, acid and pain pills on top of the alcohol, it was a deadly combination. Someone shouted that the cops were coming and everyone started running.

There were some woods across the street from the house we were at. I ran into the woods and at about that time, I started to hallucinate. I had taken acid before, but this was different. This was a bad trip. I started to run. I wasn't thinking that the police were after me, I was thinking that demons were chasing me. You know, there is no doubt in my mind that drugs are birthed straight out of the pits of Hell. There is a park in Ruston called Toma Lodge. It is more like a really up scaled flower garden. It has a high fence all the way around it. That is where I wound up. I do remember making it to the fence and trying to climb over the fence. Apparently, when I got to the top of the fence, somehow one foot made it over and my other foot didn't. The second strand from the top of the fence looped over my foot, wrapped around my ankle and left me hanging upside down. That's the last thing I remember.

When I came to, I was in the Intensive Care Unit at the hospital. My mom and dad were in the room with me. They said that I had stopped breathing on the way to the hospital and had almost died. I remember they wouldn't let me have a television set in the room. They said that when you are high on LSD that it would cause flash backs. I do remember, even 4 days after the overdose, I was still hallucinating. I stayed in the hospital about 8 days. Immediately, my parents wanted to send me to rehab. I reluctantly went to a rehab in Monroe, Louisiana called Woodland Hills. At this time, it was a really nice drug rehabilitation center with good intentions. The people were really nice and they had my best interest at heart. I remember them putting me on a drug called Librium. I didn't like it because all I did was sleep for about 4 or 5 days. They were putting me through detox. I stayed for 30 days and was released.

Within a month or so, I was using again. I met another girl and started dating her and tried to tone my drug use down. We were married and eventually, we had a baby on the way. This wife wasn't going to put up with my drug use and so I toned it down, but would still slip up while trying to control my drug use. Then, Lindsey Blake Mitchell came along, a beautiful baby girl. The apple of my eye. I had already decided that if I ever had a child, no matter if it was a boy or a girl, I was going to name her after my little brother. His name was Gregory Blake Mitchell so Lindsey was named after Greg with the name Blake as her middle name. I knew I had to stop this mess. It was time to be responsible. I had a baby girl who was awesome and now I was a daddy. And so I stopped using for about a year.

You know the scripture in the Bible that say's Bad company corrupts good character. That is such a true statement. I started running around with my old friends again and let me say this; it was not hard to talk me into using drugs. I don't blame anyone for my actions. I was grown and old enough to know better. But by this time, the drugs were starting to call my name. And not a day would pass by that I didn't think about my little brother. Now the concerns from my second wife were growing and my mom and dad had begun to really question what was going on with me. About that time, my wife told me that she was pregnant again. Logann Brooke Mitchell entered the world, another beautiful little girl. Man, what was I thinking! I have got to stop using and so I did for a little while. I played with my kids, I went to work, and I would lift weights and try to be a good husband and daddy.

I remember when they were little, I would put them in the bathtub together and we would sing our favorite songs to each other. Lindsey would always start off with her song, and then when she would finish she would say, "Your turn daddy." I would chose a song and then Logann would say, "My turn." Logann only knew one song. It was Tim McGraw's *Johnny's Daddy was Taking him Fishing*. She would sing the same phrase over and over. Lindsey and I would giggle at her. I really loved my girls. I was just not there for them like I should have been. The relationship with the girls has been strained to this very day. I dropped the ball on them and they are bitter and have every right to be. Even with 2 beautiful baby girls, I couldn't stop.

My drug use started back up and so we split up. I started using really heavy when we split up. I stayed high every day. I started running in circles with different people because my friends were starting to get concerned about me, and so I would go and hang out with people that didn't know me. In fact, I was using so much cocaine now that my nose was bleeding every time I would snort a line of coke. I started losing cartilage from inside of my nasal cavity and my eyes would swell shut. One day, I was bleeding so badly, from the coke going up my nose, that one of my buddy's said, "You should try crack. It won't affect your nasal passages." That was a really bad idea. I had found the new love of my life. Crack Cocaine.

I was getting ready to see the devil eye to eye. You know, when I first started to use crack, I would still hang around with my friends and do drugs with them. I remember one night, me and a couple of guy's drove over to the worst part of town, known as "east end." I knew a lot of the guy's that lived in the housing projects because I played ball with lots of those guy's in high school. I had joined a boxing club when I was in high school and was pretty good with my hands and so I really wasn't scared of much. The combination of that, the drugs in my system, and having an anger that was burning on the insides of me was again a deadly combination. Well, when we pulled up on a corner over on East End, there was a runner standing out there waving us down.

Now, here are three white boys in a predominantly black neighborhood sitting in a vehicle. Not very smart, but we were wanting to get high. The guy came up to my window and said, "What you want?"

I said, "A hundred of the hard." That means Crack.

He said, "Give me the money and I'll be right back."

I said, "Not happening, go get it, and we will wait on you."

So he took off. I had my window rolled down and my arm hanging out of my window and my money was cupped in the palm of my hand. I did not know that there was another guy who had come up behind my vehicle and he came up and grabbed the money out of the palm of my hand and took off running up into the projects. The guys that were with me looked at me and said, "Well there goes that."

Before I could even think, a rage came over me and I opened the door and took off running up into the projects. The guys that were with me shouted at me to get back before I got killed, but all I could think about was there goes a hundred dollars worth of crack. I ran to where I saw him last and I turned right and was not at all expecting to see him sitting there on his knees counting the money. I jumped on this guy and started pounding him. He couldn't believe that I came into the projects looking for him. Some guys ran up and pulled me off of him. For a split second, I thought I was going to die right there, but I knew two of the guys that were there. They asked me what happened. When I told them what happened, I was shocked at what happened next. They looked at the guy that took my money and said, "Yeah, you done stole from the wrong white boy this time." They actually made fun of the guy right to his face. I left unharmed. I was very blessed not to have been killed right there. I look back on the things that I did when I was so messed up, and I know with everything within me, that God was so patient with me and was always there to protect me.

I soon found myself back in another rehab called CDU of Glenwood. Another 30 days of detox. I was slowly losing touch with reality. But then something amazing happened to me. I was trying to stop drugging and I said, "That's it. I'm just going to go hang out in the bars and run with a different group of friends; friends that didn't do drugs." And so, that's what I did.

One night, I was hanging out with some friends and we were going to a karaoke bar. This girl I knew said, "Just meet me at my house, let me get a shower, and we will go out."

I said, "Okay", and while she was getting in the shower, I started looking through some of her scrap books. I came across a picture of this beautiful girl, who was in a lot of her pictures. When she came back into the living room, I said, "Laurie, who is this girl in this picture?"

She answered, "That's Leanne Lord. Why do you ask?"

I replied, "Man, she is beautiful. You need to hook a brother up!"

Laurie said, "Well, I can because her brother is married to my sister."

Laurie went back to her room and within a few minutes, the phone rang and Laurie yelled from the other room for me to answer the phone for her. I picked up the phone and said hello. The voice on the other end of the phone asked, "Is Laurie there?"

I said, "Yes, but she is in the bathroom right now. Can I give her a message for you?"

She answered, "Yes, just tell her Leanne called."

I asked, "Leanne Lord?"

"Yes, who is this?"

I said, "Don't worry about who this is, you just get yourself over to Laurie's house because we are going out tonight."

She replied, "I don't even know who this is and besides I have to work tonight."

I asked, "What do you do?"

She answered, "I'm a nurse and I work over in Monroe at Glenwood Hospital."

Unbelievable, the same hospital where I just got out of rehab. Anyway, about that time, Laurie came into the living room and I said, "Oh, here she is," and I handed her the phone. Leanne asked Laurie who the mad man on the phone was and Laurie said, "That's Keith Mitchell, he wants to meet you." Leanne ask Laurie how I knew who she was and she said that I had been looking through some pictures and thought that she was beautiful. Curiosity killed the canary. That night when Leanne got off of work, we were all back over at Laurie's and Leanne showed up. The pictures of Leanne didn't do her justice. She was the most beautiful thing that I had ever seen! Ever! But it wasn't until she opened her mouth and I heard her speak, I looked at her and knew that there was something about this girl that was different from any girl I had ever met. She had a presence about her, the way she carried herself, the way she smiled. For the next few weeks, she was all I could think about. We were inseparable.

In a time in my life where I was losing touch with reality, Leanne was put directly in the path of a major storm that was brewing. There was a big part of me that wanted to tell her about my drug problem, but I couldn't do it. All I knew was that she was the only thing in my life that seemed good and pure at the time. She made me laugh and smile and made me want to be better. We started dating and it got serious. And the whole time, it seemed like I knew that it was just a matter of time until the inevitable was going to happen, but still I hoped for the best. I really didn't want her to suffer through the madness of my addiction. I also knew that people had told her who I was and what I was capable of. Still, she loved me like I loved her. I knew without a shadow of a doubt that she was my soul mate.

We decided to get married and soon she was pregnant. Pregnant with our first child. A son! A big, blue eyed, baby boy. We named him Trevor Kade Mitchell. I had worked at the same job for a long time moving around within the company because I would work for a couple of years in one department then move to another department. I was allowed to do so because my dad had been a boss there for many years. I think they probably felt sorry for my dad because of what he had gone through losing his youngest son to a motorcycle accident and then having lost his other son to a drug addiction. I know everyone knew how bad it was, but they turned a blind eye and like my dad, they were hoping for the best. The best wasn't coming anytime soon. I went to work, then came home, and was watching my son grow up, but, within 2 years, I was back on the crack pipe.

I eventually left the job where I had worked for many years and started my own business, a decorative concrete business. I went to school down in Baton Rouge, Louisiana and poured all of my retirement funds in starting the business. It was a great business and I was the only one in town doing this kind of work. I started off doing residential work, but soon commercial contractors started calling me because they liked the work that I was doing. My company was growing very fast. I was making lots of money. At first, it was great. I was training my guys how to do the jobs and soon I had several crews working. I was rolling. I was so busy I began to get tired. I needed a pick me up. I started using Crystal Meth. It would keep me going for days. And I was smoking crack, too. I was losing weight at a rapid pace. I went from weighing 170 lbs to 130lbs almost overnight. People were starting to ask questions. Finally, I thought, *hey, I'm making a ton of money. I'll just bid the jobs and let my crews do the work. That way no one will see me and I can basically stay home and smoke crack.* And that's exactly what I did. You see, what I want you to realize is how sick and twisted your mind can get after lengthy drug use. I would stay up in my upstairs bedroom and smoke crack. Leanne always tried to shelter all 3 of my kids from seeing their daddy all messed up on dope. When it was my weekend to have the kids, she would see that I was high and she would shield the kids from seeing me like this. She would tell them over and over that I was sick and to stay down stairs.

Do you remember how I told you that I would go and like to use drugs around other people? Well now I had gotten to the point where I had become a recluse. I didn't want to see anyone, but my dealer. The pathetic thing is, I would stay up in my bedroom and smoke until it was all gone. I was too afraid to drive back across town to "east end" because the cops knew I was using. Ruston is a small town, where everyone knows everybody. There were nights when I would crawl on the carpet looking for a crumb of crack to smoke. I would be on my knees for hours looking for that crumb. Paranoia had begun to really set in on me. Leanne was no longer sleeping with me. She would sleep downstairs with the baby. I would be upstairs looking for crumbs. I can't even begin to tell you how much carpet fresh that I smoked, thinking it was crack.

It could have been 100 degrees outside and I would cut the air conditioner off inside the house because I wanted to be able to hear if someone came up to the house. I would stare out the windows for hours, not moving, thinking that they were coming to get me. Looking back now, I don't even know who they were. On one stretch, I had been up for about 3 days straight and I took a bunch of valiums one night to try and come down from all of the crack. Twice in my life, I have heard an audible voice coming from somewhere other than this world we live in. The first time it happened was on this night. I had been smoking crack for 3 days and I had just started to doze off when, in a very real and weird voice, I heard someone whisper into my ear, "I've got you. You will never quit." I jumped up off of the bed scared to death. A couple of nights later, I was asleep and dreaming. Have you ever been having a really bad dream and you feel like someone is in the room with you, but you can't scream. That is what was happening to me. I looked up and saw this huge black wave coming towards me and it was moving at least 500 mph. All of a sudden, it came into the bedroom, stopped, and when it did I felt something standing right beside me. I turned my head and there was standing right to the side of my bed was a black mass. It was not your normal black. It was the darkest black figure I had ever seen. I tried and tried to scream. I wanted to move my arms, but I couldn't move. That dream stayed with me forever and I have a pretty good idea who it was that was in the room with me. I will tell you about the second voice later in the book. It was a lot different of a voice.

Leanne soon gave me an ultimatum, either go back to rehab or she was leaving. I soon went back to rehab. This time it was in Rayville, Louisiana. I guess I need to mention that there were several outpatient clinics that I had to attend as well. Anyway, this rehab in Rayville is called Palmetto. I was there for about 45 days and then released. I knew Leanne was who I was supposed to be with, so I went back home and tried to be good. Leanne was raised Methodist and so we went to church at Trinity Methodist Church. It is located on the I-20 service road in Ruston. That is where my little brother Greg was killed, right in front of the church. An old man of 76 failed to see him coming down the service road and pulled out in front of him. His name was Mr. Wallace. He was the custodian at the church. I'm not going to lie. I was really angry at Mr. Wallace for a long time. I was mad because he never called my mom or dad to check on them, to see if they were okay. I found out, many years later, that the reason he never came and checked on my mom and dad is because he couldn't. They said he was a sweet old man and that it would have killed him. I feel really bad now because I harbored such anger in my heart for him. He passed away many years ago. I know Greg and I'm sure that he has had plenty of time in Heaven to tell Mr. Wallace that it's okay and that it was an accident.

We started going to church at Trinity and we had ties at that church. Although we never went to church often when we were kids, we would go on their summer trips with the youth group. The prettiest girls in town went to church there and so we would go with them. One year, we went to Petijean Mountain in Arkansas. There were probably 60 to 70 kids on the trip. Greg and I both went on this trip. He was 16 and I was 17. One night, the youth director, Wallace Martin, was speaking and asks if anyone wanted to have Jesus come into their life. There were several kids going down to the front to accept Christ as their personal savior. Greg got up and instead of walking down to the front, he turned around and came and got me. He said, "Keith, I don't know how to pray. Would you go down front and pray with me?" I didn't know how to pray either, but reluctantly I got up and went down there with him. As we got down to the front, one of the counselors, Mrs. Charlotte Durrett, came over to us and asked Greg if he wanted to say the sinner's prayer. He said yes and gave his heart to the Lord. I wasn't quite ready to, but I sure was happy for Greg. After he died, that was the only thing that I could think about was that night up in Arkansas.

Leanne and I started attending Trinity Church. It kept Leanne happy and I was still secretly smoking crack. I am really ashamed of this, because several times I even had my dealer pull into the church parking lot and leave me some dope in the cars glove compartment. I would leave the money in the ash tray for him, but boy I sure thought I had everyone fooled. I didn't understand the sermons. I didn't know anything about the Bible, but when Church was over, I would shake everyone's hand and smile really big and wave at everybody. Looking back, I know that the joke was on me. These brothers and sisters were in the house of God worshipping the Almighty God. They had peace and joy in their lives and meanwhile, I was dying a slow death. It's like when you are hooked on dope, you get tunnel vision. The cravings are so severe that it's all you can think about.

The other day, I was watching T.V. and flipping through the channels when I came across the show Intervention. It's a show about people who are hooked on drugs and the family has to have an Intervention. I'm glad no one was at home with me because I began to weep watching the pain that this Mom and Dad were going through. You could see how much they loved their child and they said they had lost her and they knew that she was going to die. I knew that look. I had seen it a thousand times in my own mother's eyes. My Mom used to cry and sit and ask me why I couldn't stop. And all I could say to her was, "Mom, I'm sorry. I don't know why." I would cry with her and tell her how sorry I was. And she would pray. The prayers of a mother are a powerful thing let me tell you, and my mom wasn't even saved at the time. But she still cried out to God, "Please help my son." I would hear her pray that and it would kill me. I would want to die. I can't tell you how many times I held a gun to my mouth and wanted so badly to pull the trigger. I couldn't do it. Each time, I would see my children's faces, Leanne's, and my Mom and dad's faces. I just couldn't do it. I think in the back of my dad's mind he knew that I might kill myself because from time to time he would say, "No matter how bad it gets, you know suicide is the cowards way out."

I knew he was just scared. My Dad quit drinking when Greg and I were just little boys. He came home drunk one night and passed out on the floor. I saw him and started to cry. That started Greg crying. We said, "Momma, daddy's dead!"

She said, "He's not dead; he's drunk. That' where he will stay until tomorrow." The next morning, Dad woke up and saw Greg lying in one of his arms and me in the other.

When he saw that, he said he would never drink again. And he didn't. And so, I couldn't understand why I couldn't stop. Dad did it. Why can't I? The anger started to really build up in me. I hated the man that I saw in the mirror, a weak and pathetic loser. Maybe that voice I had heard in my bedroom that night was right. I couldn't stop, and I was going to die. I had already lost several of my close friends due to drug overdoses.

I had begun taking my money, everything that I was earning and spent it on crack. I was even spending Kades diaper money in the crack house. Eventually, the inevitable happened. Leanne left me. Actually, she kicked me out. I didn't have any where to go, so I went to stay with my Mom and Dad. They wanted that anyway. That's when my addiction went into warp speed. I would go and get the crack and drive down the country roads for hours. We had a hunting lease in Jackson parish and I would drive down there and pull onto one of our dirt roads and hide my truck. It was in the middle of the summer and in Louisiana it's hot all the time. I would cut off my engine and sit there for hours sweating like a pig smoking crack. I would get a couple of packs of cigarettes and a couple of bottles of water. Sometimes, I would be without water for 7 or 8 hours and after 2 or 3 days of binging, my body would begin to cramp up. I had lost weight down to about 125 lbs. I looked really bad.

One night, I was riding out in the country and I had just hit the pipe while I was driving. I had taken a huge hit off of the pipe and when I looked up, there was a car pulling out of a driveway. I stopped suddenly and swerved off of the road. The car in front of me took off and I hit something in the road. I thought I heard a cop saying, "Stop the car." I was completely freaked out. I sped up and I could tell that I was dragging something under my vehicle and I thought it was the cop. I never stopped. I just kept going. I must have been driving 90 mph. I drove around for about an hour and it was now about 2 in the morning. I went back by the house where I thought I had run someone over and found out what I was dragging, it was their trash can. I was really scared to drive after that because I was afraid I was going to kill someone. I needed to come up with a different plan. From that point on, I either rented a hotel room or I would just go to a crack house and stay for 2 or 3 days at a time.

My life was over. I had lost my children, the Love of my life, and my business. I had already completely lost touch with reality. John 10:10 says *The devil comes only to kill, steal, and to destroy.* And he had managed to do that with my life. But the crazy thing was, I was still mad at God, myself and whoever else would try and help me. My poor mother was trying to do whatever she could to get me some help. She called a really good friend of mine who was a dare officer with the Ruston police department. His name is Russ Thompson. Russ was a friend to me and Greg both. Russ went to high school with both of us. Russ would come over and he would talk to me as a really good friend. Russ would tell me, "Mitch, I believe in you buddy. You can do this. You have got to stop doing this. You know, Greg wouldn't want to see you like this. It's killing your mom and dad." His talks would give me hope temporarily, but I would cave in and go and use again.

One night, I was in a crack house that I wasn't familiar with. There were probably 5 or 6 guys inside the house smoking crack. I didn't know any of them. I went in with the intention of only smoking about 50 dollars worth, but after about 3 or 4 trips out to my truck, they realized I had a lot more money in the truck. I could see them peering out the windows when I would go out and get more money. Once back inside, I was hitting the pipe and I looked up and saw them whispering to each other. I acted like I didn't see it, and watched as 2 of the guys came over and sat directly behind me. I knew at that moment I was in trouble. There was no doubt that they were going to either knock me in the head or just cut my throat right there. I stood up real quick and looked at the dope man and said, "Hey man, have you got about 500 dollars worth here on you?"

He asked, "Why?"

I replied, "Because I came here to smoke and I'm tired of walking back and forth to my truck. Have you got the dope here?"

He said, "Yeah I got it, go and get your money brother."

I said, Okay," and walked out of the house. Once I was on the porch, I reached in my pocket for my keys. I got in the truck and I couldn't get out of there fast enough. There is no doubt in my mind what was getting ready to happen in that crack house. I had to do something different from then on.

There was a guy that I went to school with that didn't live on "east end" he lived on what is known as "the hike". Don't ask me, that's just what it's called. This was a guy that lived off of the beaten path. He even had a room where I would go in and stay for days on end. No one was ever in this room but me. In fact, he didn't let anyone use in his house, but me. I could hide my truck behind his house and no one could see me. He would have for me a carton of cigarettes and a case of water waiting when I got there. I had the perfect setup. This rocked on for months and my parents were horrified at my weight loss and they never knew where I was. They thought that any day I was going to turn up dead. Finally, the sheriff's department showed up at my house one afternoon and severed me with divorce paper's. Leanne had filed for a divorce. I went into a tail spin. My cousin, who lives in Lafayette and was going through a divorce at the time, knew that I was in trouble, so he came up and said for me to come and live with him for a while. He said it would do us both some good, and I thought, you know what? He is probably right. So, I packed up and moved to South Louisiana.

A couple of my best friends in Ruston, Michael and Van, were talking with each other when they found out that I had moved to Lafayette. Michael said that this looked like it was the end of the road for me. He said, "Van, I don't think that we will ever see him again. I think he will die in Lafayette." I didn't find out about their conversation until a few years later. My cousins had lived in Lafayette all of their lives and I was really close to both of them. I was the oldest of the three of us, and the younger one" Tony", and I had gotten closer through the years because we shared a lot of the same interests. We just spent more time together. Randy and I were really close too, but he had just opened up a new bar and was busy with that. I needed money and so I helped out at the club a few nights a week. What I didn't realize was how crazy the night life was in Lafayette. I stayed out all night just about every night.

Tony and I shared an apartment and we were both single and going crazy. Tony had lived there all of his life and his parents had been in the night club business for years. So Tony knew tons of people down there. He was in his 30's and was a great looking guy. He had a bunch of really cool guys that he hung around with. We were bringing home different ladies every night. His friends liked me because I was T's cousin. They had no idea about my deep dark secret. Tony and his buddy's drank and went out. None of it was a good thing. I'm just saying that they were not anywhere close to being where I was at with my problem. I couldn't let those guys know how bad my problem was. Tony kind of knew, but wasn't aware of how bad it really was.

Well, one night, they all went out of town to Baton Rouge which is about 45 minutes to an hour from Lafayette. Randy had asked me to give him a hand at his club that night and so I went to help Randy out. Randy's help finally showed up about 3 in the morning, so I was going to call it a night and go home. I was driving back to the apartment and stopped at a convenience store for a pack of smokes. There was a guy who was having problems with his car. His battery was dead, so I gave him a jump. He asked, "How much do I owe you?"

I could tell that he was high and so I said, "How about a line?"

He replied, "You ain't the Po Po are you?"

I started laughing, I said, Naw man, I ain't the police."

He said, "What you looking for?"

I said, "Some powder (that's Cocaine)."

He replied, "I got a little something. Pull around on the side of the store."

I got out of my vehicle and got in his. He said, "I got some powder and a little bit of 'h'." He was talking about heroin. He asked, "Have you ever speed balled before?"

I said, "No. I've banged coke before, but never speed balled before." To" bang it" means to mainline the drugs into your veins. And a speedball is when you mix the cocaine and heroin together and shoot it. Your system doesn't know what to do because cocaine is an upper and heroin is a downer. Well, I said, "No I haven't, but there is no time like the present."

He said, "I have got some brand new points." I watched him pull them out. I had shot dope before, but I was always really scared of using someone else's needle. And so I was really glad to see that they were individually wrapped. Once he got it ready, he hit me with it. It was a different high than I had ever felt. It was not like shooting cocaine; it was kind of mellow. The only way I can describe it is that it was like a train insulated with marsh mellows had hit me. They had always told me, before I ever shot cocaine for the first time, that as soon as you pulled the needle out of your arm, you could hear a train coming and they were right. I stayed in touch with this guy and he became my heroin connection. For the record, my Cousin Tony has since given his life to the Lord and is a devout Christian man who has gotten married and has a beautiful wife, and four beautiful little girls.

I called my dealer back in Ruston and asked him if he wanted some "h." He said heck yeah and maybe we could trade some out. That is what I was looking for because I could charge him 3 times what I paid for it and could speed ball all I wanted for free. This rocked on for a while. I was making trips back and forth from Lafayette to Ruston. I would get to see Kade when I went home. By this time, Leanne couldn't stand the sight of me. The girls had moved to Orange, Texas with their mother and I was now officially the "father of the century". Honestly, I was useless and I knew it. I would lie awake at night and think about how screwed up I had become. Where were all the people that I loved? What were they doing right now? Were the kids okay? Was Leanne with someone else by now? How were my Mom and Dad? ... I'm Pathetic! ... Loser! ... You are right where you deserve to be! ... Alone! ... Unhappy! The voice I heard that night was true! I'm going to die doing this. My only hope, at this point, was that someone other than a family member would find me, if I were to die of an overdose.

Well, this one trip back to Ruston I called my dealer and asked him if he had some powder. He said no, but he had all the Crack that I could smoke. I left Lafayette and headed back to Ruston. I never even called my Mom or Dad to let them know I was coming to town. Once I arrived in town, I drove over to the dealer's house. I blew the horn and he came outside. As he walked up to me I said, "Hey bro, you got the dope?"

He replied, "Yeah man, I got it." He said, "Mitch! I got to ask you a favor brother."

I asked, "Yeah, what's up my man?"

He answered, "If I give you something, will you promise me you will read it?"

I said, "What are you talking about?"

He replied, "This little bible!"

I said, "What, are you kidding me?" Actually, there were some expletives thrown in there. Of course, you have to remember this is before I was born again. I said, "What the heck are you thinking man? Do you see anything remotely wrong with this picture?" I looked at him and said, "Bro, don't you ever do this to me again."

He said, "Mitch, it's just that you ain't the same old brother from back in the day man. You was one of those white boys that all the brother's liked because you was straight and didn't take nothing off of anybody. Look at you now man! You don't even way 130 lbs." And then he said something that hit me hard. He said, "Brother, I don't think you gonna be around long. I think you need to read that book." It was a Gideon's bible that he found in a hotel room.

I said, "Hey man, give me the dope."

He handed me both. I threw the Bible on the back seat and drove away. I was angry. How could he even have the audacity to think he could give me a Bible? He was a drug dealer for crying out loud. Are you kidding me! I drove over to an old cheap hotel in Ruston. I asked if I could have a room in the very back. It was secluded back there, away from the highway and the noise. I had just picked up about a thousand dollars worth of crack. I had a bottle of wine and a bottle of valium. The smoking session had begun. For 24 hours, I smoked nonstop. I had run out of cigarettes and needed some water, so I drove down to a convenience store and went in looking all crazy. I know the clerk could tell I was all messed up, so I bought 5 packs of smokes and 3 or 4 bottles of water and went back to the room. I smoked until dark and realized I was going to run out of crack, so I called my dealer. He said he would bring some more over to the room and he did. I smoked all night and all the next day. My chest started pounding and I knew I needed to come down because my heart was fluttering. I took a few valium, turned up the bottle of wine and drank as much as I could.

I began to get really paranoid; my dealer was the only one who knew where I was at. I looked out of the window continually and, hour after hour, I was getting more and more paranoid. I went to the window and saw a van sitting outside my room and it had a satellite on top and then it hit me. I was being set up. The task force was out there and they were going to bust me. It had to be my dealer. He was the only one who knew where I was at. It was beginning to make sense now. He tried to give me the Bible and now I know why, he did it because he was feeling guilty. Man, I will tell you something, when you have been up for that many hours, your mind starts playing tricks on you. Your mind races a million miles an hour and you always think the worst, especially when dope is involved. I started to panic. I knew that the task force knew that I had been bringing heroin into town. This is it. I'm going down right here. I looked up about that time and I saw something that looked like a piece of flex hose coming through the air-conditioning vent in my hotel room. They were watching me now from inside the room. I ran to the bathroom. As I shut the door, I heard them crawling through the attic scrambling to get to the bathroom. I hurriedly loaded my pipe and took the biggest hit that I could. As soon as I exhaled, I could hear them trying to come through the front door. I tried to flush what I could down the toilet, but what I didn't realize is that it didn't go down. Pipe and about three hundred dollars worth of crack were still in the toilet. I ran out of the bathroom and turned left. I could hear them come in the front and so I ran as hard as I could and jumped out of the back window. I hit the ground and got up running. There were nothing but woods behind my room, and so I took off down through the woods as fast as I could run. I was running down hill through the woods and was looking back over my shoulder and I could see flashlights coming my way. As I turned around, I ran face first into a huge oak tree. I hit the tree so hard it knocked me completely out. The impact was so hard that both of my tennis shoes came off. I don't know how long I was unconscious. I do vaguely remember coming to and thinking wow it has started to rain, but something was different. I felt really weird. It wasn't rain; it was blood that had covered my face. All I was wearing was a pair of khaki shorts and a sweatshirt. I was now barefoot and it was the middle of December. It was cold. I got up and started to run. I ran through the woods and ran through a barb wire fence. It cut my chest and tore my sweat shirt. I kept running. I crossed a road that was usually pretty busy, but got across unnoticed. I came to the railroad tracks and ran down the tracks as fast as I could. What I didn't realize is that people love to break beer bottles and such along the tracks. I don't know if it was all the glass and all those jagged rocks that were on the tracks, but my feet were being cut to pieces. I was beginning to feel really weird. I remember hearing dogs barking while I was crawling up the side of a hill. I thought, *Aw man, they have turned the dogs loose on me.* Then, I could see the guys from the task force closing in on me. They were trying to surround me and I could literally see them crouching down and closing in. I jumped up and ran up the hill into a neighborhood. I crawled under a house. I don't know how long I was there because I lost consciousness. When I came to, I remember thinking, *Man these people must have a water leak* because I was soaking wet, my head was soaked and I could tell my feet were lying in a pool of water. Only it wasn't water, it was blood. I crawled out from under the house and tried to stand to my feet. I couldn't. That scared me. I crawled over to a fence and pulled myself up. I remember that I couldn't get my legs under me. I had been hit hard in the ring, but never anything like this. As I slowly began to walk, I could actually feel my legs coming back. Soon, I was trotting down the street.

There was a dealer, I would use from time to time, who lived just right down the street from where I was. I used him when my guy would run out. I made it to his house and rang his doorbell. When he answered the door, he jumped backwards with a really shocked look. It took him a few seconds to recognize who I was. I hadn't seen myself, so I had no idea how bad I looked. I had no idea that my eyes were almost completely swollen shut, and for the first time, I looked down and could see my feet. I knew that they were in really bad shape. He opened the door and said, "Man, what happened? Were you in a wreck?"

I replied, "No man, the Law is after me."

He said, "Yo man, get up out of my house man. I got all kinda stuff in here man, you gotta go dawg."

That made me mad. I said, "Hey man, after all the money I've spent over here with you, you can't even give me a ride somewhere. Forget you brother, I'll be back bro, and we will get this straight."

I don't know if he actually felt bad or if he just got scared that a raving lunatic was just standing under his car port bleeding to death, threatening to come back and squash this at a later date, because as I was walking through his back-yard, he ran around the corner of his house and yelled with a whisper, "Mitch, c'mon man. I'll give you a ride man."

Even when I was bleeding almost to death, pride still got in the way. I turned to him, shouted a few expletives at him, and told him I would die first before he would give me a ride anywhere. And I was on my way again. At this point, I didn't know really what to do. I was in the very middle of town. How was I going to get to where I needed to be? I didn't even know where I was going. I thought Leanne was at work. She worked in the emergency room at the hospital as a Registered Nurse, so I decided I could go to her house because I still had a key to the house. Now, if I could only find my way. My Dad's office was just down the road. I knew that the rail road tracks were right there. I could figure it all out when I got there, so I just kept walking. By this time, my feet were really hurting bad. I looked up and there was a guy standing at his car putting a towel across his windshield because it was so cold he was trying to keep ice from forming on his windshield. I walked up behind him and said, "Excuse me sir." When he turned around and saw my face, the first thing out of his mouth was, "Oh my God. Are you okay?"

I said, "Yeah, I'm okay."

He asked, "Were you in a wreck?" And he started looking back up the road to see if he could see any wrecked vehicles. He said, "Man, you really need a hospital. Let me call you an ambulance."

I said, "No! Please don't call one. I'll be okay. I just need some socks or a pair of old shoes. I'll pay you for them."

He responded, "That's okay," and walked back to his house. As he got to the front door, his wife came out and screamed, "Oh my God, what happened?"

He said, "Honey, this gentleman has been in a wreck and he needs some shoes."

She had a really puzzled look on her face and then she said, "Let me call you an ambulance."

I said, "No! Please don't call an ambulance."

Her husband returned with a pair of old sneakers. I said thank you and took off walking. When they shut the door, I started running. I made it down the street to my dad's office where I slipped on the old sneakers. Man they felt good on my feet. I made it to the railroad tracks and started walking. I was coming up on Railroad Park in Ruston. The railroad tracks ran right though the middle of town. Now what was I going to do? I had an idea that, at the time, seemed like a good idea. There was a bar in the middle of town right beside the railroad tracks. One of my best buddy's was a regular patron at this local pub. I thought, *You know what I will take a chance and go in and see if he is there.* When I walked through those doors, it's as if time stood still. There were people shooting pool and people gathered around the bar. Ruston is a college town and it was like Greek night there. Usually, it is a place for older Ruston locals, but not this night. Nope, no such luck. I didn't know a soul. People rushed up to me and were asking me if I was alright. I thought, *Man these people sure are making a huge fuss.* They asked me if I had been in a wreck and I had just replied yes. They asked me where and I just said I couldn't remember. They wanted to call me an ambulance and they were going to and so I ask if anyone knew Tony Farley. A couple of people knew Tony and said, Yeah, he just left."

I asked," Can you guys call him? He will come and get me and he will take me to the hospital." They agreed and called Tony. Tony was one of my oldest and dearest friends. Tony had never taken a drug in his life and was just a really good guy. This guy approached me and ask if he could buy me a beer while a was waiting on Tony? I said sure. He sat and stayed with me until Tony arrived at the bar. Once Tony made it to the table, Tony said, "My God Mitch, we need to get you to a hospital."

I said, "I'm okay Tony. I'm just glad to see you, just take me home."

Tony looked at the guy sitting there with me and said, "Has he seen himself in the mirror?"

The guy replied, "I don't think so."

They got me to my feet and walked me to the men's room. Once I looked into the mirror, I didn't even recognize myself. It was a lot worse than I could have imagined. As I stood there looking into the mirror, I remembered the conversation a couple of days earlier with the dealer when he said, "I don't think your gonna be here long." Then I started thinking about the voice again. I got you! You will never quit! I knew I was in a bad spot. Maybe I was ready for it all to be over. We walked out of the bar and we got into Tony's car. Tony started driving towards the hospital. When we were getting close to the hospital, I said, "Tony, take a right here at this red light."

Tony said, "Mitch, the hospital is on the left."

I said, "I'm not going to the hospital."

He said, "What?"

I explained, "Tony, I got set up tonight by my drug dealer. I'm going to go set this straight with him."

Tony said, "Man, have you lost your mind?"

I replied, "Tony, you know me. Once my mind is made up, there is nothing anyone can do to talk me out of it."

Tony stopped the car and said, "Mitch, you need a hospital. I'm telling you, you are going to be dead before daylight." He drove me over to the dealer's house. The dealer had a long driveway. The porch light was on and there were 5 or 6 guys outside on the porch. Tony said, "This is the stupidest thing you have ever done." I think Tony was really mad at me and himself, for not just driving on to the hospital. As I was getting out of his car, he said, "Mitch, don't do this."

I replied," Don't worry, I will be fine."

Tony drove away and I started walking up the long drive way. As I walked from out of the darkness and into the light coming from his porch, the guys that were standing on his porch could see me by now. They could see I was white and really messed up. They said, "Hey man, you got company out here. We are out of here man!" They walked passed me without saying a word. About that time the dealer came to the door and saw that it was me, he pushed his screen door open and grabbed me and started pulling me inside his house.

He said, "Mitch, what happened man?"

I replied, "I don't know, brother. You tell me."

He said, "I don't know what you are talking about, man."

I responded, "Really? You are the only person that knew where I was, man."

He said, "Mitch, man, what you trying to say brother?"

I answered, "All I know is the task force came in on me tonight and you are the only person that knew where I was at."

He asked, "Man, are you being for real?"

I replied, Look at me, man. What do you think?"

He answered, "Look man, I've been knowing you since elementary school. You're my boy. Why would I do that? Mitch, tell me what happened?"

I told him everything and he looked at me and said, "Mitch, are you sure that the task force was after you?"

I sat there for what seemed like forever staring at the floor. The dope was wearing off. I knew it because I was in severe pain. I looked at him and said, "There wasn't even anybody there, was it?"

He replied, "Naw man. Mitch, that's why I gave you that Bible, man. Look bro," he said, "you are in trouble. You gotta stop this madness for a while, Mitch. You gotta go to the hospital."

I said, "Look man, I ain't going to the hospital. Look man, I'm hurting really bad. Give me a hundred dollars worth."

He replied, "Man, you done lost your mind."

I said, "Look man, I have spent all this money. I am hurting and I need something."

He said, "Man, I'm gonna give you this, but you can't stay here." So he gave me the crack and drove me over to Leanne's house. I got out and went in the house. I had no idea that every time I would take a step, blood was running out of the sneakers that I had been given earlier. I went up the stairs and walked all over the house leaving a trail of blood everywhere I went. I finally went into the downstairs bathroom where I shut the door. I had smoked about half of the crack and had finally lost consciousness. My cousin Tony, his Mom and his dad had just so happened to drive to Ruston to see my folks. Apparently, when Tony had made it home, his wife asked him about me and he told her the story. She said, "Tony! You have got to call Lefty."

Lefty is my Dad! So Tony called my Dad and told him what happened and that I was in trouble. Well, Tony drove over and he, my Dad, my cousin, and my uncle went to the drug dealer's house. My dad has never mentioned to me anything that was said over at the dealer's house. But Tony and my uncle have told me that my dad got out of the car, walked up to the door and said, "Where is my son?"

The dealer said, "Mr. Mitchell, I drove him over to his ex-wife's house and dropped him off.

They said that my dad told him, "I have buried one of my boys and he was the baby, and if you sell the only son I have left any more dope, your people will be burying you."

I felt bad because no one was twisting my arm to make me use drugs. I know that my Dad was at the end of his rope and he loves me so much that it was killing him. When they got to Leanne's house, they found me lying on the floor unconscious and foaming at the mouth. My dad had stopped by his house and picked up my Mom and my aunt. I wished he wouldn't have. When I came to, I was in the ICU unit. They worked on me until daylight sewing me up. I had lost a lot of blood. They said if I had I not gotten to the hospital when I did, I would have died. I wound up having to have stitches to the front and back of my head. I had to have 50 stitches in one foot and 70 stitches in the other. The bad thing was the next morning, Leanne came into work and her co-workers had to tell her that I was in ICU. She never came to see me! By this time, she was so embarrassed and ashamed that she had ever married me. She wanted absolutely nothing to do with me. Could you blame her?

After a few days in the ICU, they moved me into a regular room. My mom and dad were there. It was really horrible that my parents had witnessed what they did. My mother worked at the hospital in the medical records department. I'm sure it was very embarrassing for her. Everyone loved my mom because she always greeted everyone with a warm and friendly smile. She was a very sweet and kind woman. After a few days, my folks had to go back to work. There was a rumor that went around town that I was beaten within an inch of my life by a bunch of drug dealers. Lots of people came by the hospital to see me. I know the real reason a lot of them came by was to just gawk at how bad my face looked. A lot of my friends came by and cried at my bedside and begged me to stop using. We had just lost one of our closest friends to cancer. He died on November 5th, my Birthday. I had been a pallbearer at his funeral. To be quite honest, at this point, I really didn't care one way or the other if I lived or died. The latter sounded a whole lot better at the time.

After everyone left, I called the dealer and had him bring fifty dollars worth of crack to my hospital room. He was scared to death that my Dad was gonna find out and was going to kill him. He brought it anyway. I sat and smoked the crack in my hospital room. After I got out of the hospital, I went back to my mom and dad's house. After a couple of days, when I was beginning to heal up, I was sitting on my dad's back patio when he came out and sat down. Dad said, "Son, you are killing us. Your mom is going to have a nervous breakdown." Someone at the hospital had given my Mom a copy of a book called "Tuff Love." I've hated that book for ever. I have not read the book, but I know that any parent or loved one, who is an enabler to someone who is hooked on drugs, should read this book. And this is the reason I say this. My Mom and Dad, my ex wives, and many of my friends were caught in the trap of feeling sorry for me.

Listen, Drug addicts are manipulators. They are con artist. I say they because I am no longer bound by those chains of addiction. I have been set free by the blood of Jesus Christ. Romans 6:17-18, *But Thanks be to God that, though you used to be slaves to sin, you whole heartedly obeyed the form of teaching to which you were entrusted. You have been set free of sin and have become slaves to righteousness.* My Mom said she wasn't going to enable me for another second. Honestly, they should have taken that stance long before, but they couldn't. I know it's hard to tell someone you love "no!" Believe me, you are only doing them and yourself more harm. It will actually prolong their addiction. Enablers are caught in a trap. The drug addict is going to throw a guilt trip on you every time. That is a fact. Remember, they are con-artists and manipulators. Pro's at playing on your sympathy. I know because I was the best at doing that. My Mom shed so many tears through the years. No one should have to endure the heartache of addiction, because so many people in each family suffer from their addiction. My Dad asked me to leave his house and not comeback. I know my Dad. And I know that was the hardest thing he has ever had to do in his life, except for when he walked into the operating room at the hospital and saw the lifeless body of his youngest child lying on the operating table. I honored my Dad's wishes because I knew he was right. Every time I watched my mom cry, it broke my heart, but I always continued to use. I used because I couldn't stop! Where had those days of innocence gone? I knew, deep down, I would never get my life back on track. I had been through to many rehabs. There was really no hope for me. I started using back in 1982. It was now 2003 and after all these years, I knew that I was getting close to either an episode I would not recover from, or I was getting really close to committing suicide.

Leanne was living her life and didn't want to even know of my whereabouts. I knew this girl in Ruston that I had dated years back. She was going through a divorce and had a couple of children. She and I had started talking and we began to see each other. After a couple of weeks, I moved in to her house. She was a very good hearted and sweet girl. She had no idea that I was as screwed up as I was. I mean, she knew I had problems with drugs, but I was about to blow her mind. I remember one night she walked into the bathroom. I thought I had locked the door. I had a crack pipe in my mouth and I had a needle hanging out of my arm. I was using heroin again and was starting to feel the heroin calling my name just like the crack did. She really cared deeply for me, and it broke her heart to see that. She knew that I had been on a four or five day binge. She fell on the floor and started crying. She said, "Don't you know that you are dying! Why can't you see that you are killing yourself? Everybody sees it, but you!"

I didn't tell her that I knew it, too! A couple of days passed and she came in the house and said, "Keith, I don't want to push you, but I can't do this anymore."

I had only been there for a month or two and I was done! I was tired and I was ready to end my time here on this earth. I was at the point that I was so angry at what I had allowed myself to become. I hated a God that I didn't even know. God was an easy target to hate. He was who I blamed outwardly. But on the inside, deep down, I blamed myself and I knew the anger came from within. How could I hate God when I didn't even know Him?

This girl asked me if I would go and talk to her pastor. I started laughing. She started to cry and walked off. I walked up to her and said, "Look, if it will make you feel better, I will go and see him." A little while later, she came and told me that her pastor would see me first thing in the morning. The next morning, she woke me up and said for me to get ready to go to the church. I got ready and we drove to the church. The Pastor's name is Bo Nicholson. He pastors

Cathedral of Praise in Ruston. He is a very soft spoken and nice gentleman. We sat down and started talking about all the drugs I was using. It was the usual type of conversation that I went through when I was sent for consultation when seeking counsel for my addiction. blah blah blah dat dat dat. Brother Bo could see that I was ready to bolt. That is when he hit me with some really tuff questions. He said, "Keith, how long have you been using drugs?"

I answered, "Since 1982."

He asked, "How many times have you been married?"

I replied, "Three times."

He inquired, "How many kids do you have?"

I said, "Three kids."

I knew that this guy was very serious. He said, "Keith, I know a place you can go, but it's a yearlong program. It's called Teen Challenge. I have heard nothing, but great things about this place."

I paused for a second and said, "Well brother Bo, I appreciate your help here, but I think we are done with this conversation."

He asked, "Why is that Keith?"

I answered, "Because I ain't about to go and stay anywhere for a year. Man, I have been in and out of so many rehabs I can't even count them. Man, rehab doesn't work."

I started to get up and he said, "Just let me ask you one more question Keith."

I said, "Okay brother Bo, Shoot!"

He replied, "Keith, are you telling me that after three failed marriages, losing your three babies, losing your health, your career, and losing many friendships, that you mean to tell me that you can't chance giving up one year of your life when you have just spent over the last twenty destroying it. Is that what you are saying Keith?"

He really hit a cord with me. I was so mad when I walked out of his office, as mad as could be. We walked to the car and she asked, "What do you think?"

I replied, "I think you are both nuts! That's what I think."

She drove me back to her house and dropped me off because she had to go to work. I jumped in my truck and drove to east end. I picked up about fifty dollars worth of crack and that led to another, then another by time she got home that evening, I was in really bad shape. When she got home, I figured she was going to go crazy, but she didn't. Later that night, I was lying there thinking about my three kids and what a horrible dad I was. I really hated the fact that they were going to grow up knowing that everyone in town knew that their daddy was known as the worst drug addict that ever lived in that town. I told her to call Brother Bo and see if I could get into Teen Challenge. The next day, there were calls made to the Greater New Orleans Teen Challenge. Once confirmed that there was in fact a bed open, Brother Bo called and I went and had another conference with him. He gave me the phone number to the Center and gave me the name of the Intake Director there at the New Orleans Center. I had to be there in two days. I called Leanne and told her what was going on. She didn't take me serious and said, "Yeah sure, Keith. I know you are going to go and stay at this place for a whole year. Yeah, right, whatever," and she hung up.

I called my Mom and told her about Teen Challenge. I could hear in her voice the excitement because this was the first time that I ever willingly decided to go anywhere. My Mother wanted the name and number to Teen Challenge; she also wanted the Intake Director's name as well. His name is Stanley Simeon; a super wonderful man of God that I still look to for Godly council even to this very day. I called Leanne back afterwards and told her that I wanted to see Kade before I left because I wouldn't be able to see him for a really long time. She said, "So what! You don't ever see him now." I hadn't made a whole lot of attempts to see him. I knew she was right. I loved my kids so much. It penetrated to the very core of my heart, but she was right. I was the most selfish person in the world. I was married to the dope and crack cocaine and heroin were my babies. She said, "You know what Keith, I will bring him over there in the morning and let you see him before you leave for New Orleans." That night I packed for Teen Challenge not knowing what to expect.

The next morning, Leanne showed up at this girl's house and I went outside and there was my little curly haired, blue eyed boy that had a huge smile on his face when he saw his daddy standing in the driveway. He jumped out, ran to me and hugged me. I hugged him and he asked me how long I was going to be gone. Before I could reply, Leanne said, "Don't worry, Kade. He will be back in a couple of days, or a week or two." Leanne was a scorned woman. As we stood there talking, I looked up at Leanne and she was more beautiful than ever. We talked for a little while and Kade asked me why I had to go away. I told him I was really sick and I had to try and get better. He said, "Daddy, get better." I told him that I loved him to and I would see him soon. She strapped Kade in his car seat and walked over to me and said, "You know what Keith? You have completely broken my heart. Please don't hurt your little boy anymore than what he and your two little girls have already been hurt. You know, I loved you more than anything in the world, but you completely destroyed my love for you. Keith, I hope you get your life together for your children's sake," and she drove away.

Within a few minutes, my mom and dad drove up. I loaded my stuff into their vehicle, the girl I was staying with wanted to go down to New Orleans and see firsthand what the center looked like. We made the five and a half hour drive down to New Orleans. As we started to try and figure out, by the directions we were given, how to get there, we realized we were in a pretty bad part of town. I remember my mom saying, "Oh my Lord! I hope this place isn't down here."

Well, it was! It was on Franklin Avenue, right in the middle of the "lower ninth ward." Thank the Lord that my mom didn't know what the lower 9th was at the time or I would have never been dropped off at Teen Challenge. Once we were at the center, we found a place to park. We went inside where I met Brother Stanley Simeon for the first time. He was a really nice guy that gave us a tour of the facility. It was nothing like those resorts for rehabs I had stayed at in the past. I didn't think I was going to last three days at this place. Brother Stanley showed us the down stairs where basically was just the dining hall, kitchen and a chapter room that was connected to the dining hall. After that, he took us upstairs where we saw the classroom, the living quarters, the showers, which were very small, and the blessing closet upstairs for guys that came in and didn't have any clothes. There was also a small weight room there. About that time, I said, "Stanley, where do I go to smoke at? Is there a designated area?"

His reply was, "Brother Stanley."

I said, "Excuse me."

He explained, "We call everyone Brother here. That's what we are in God's eyes, Brother Keith. You will be Brother Keith the whole time you are here."

I started laughing. He never cracked a smile. I thought, *Oh My Gosh! He is serious.*

Then he said, "Brother Keith, this is a discipleship ministry. There is no smoking here at the center."

I looked at my mom and dad and they thought for sure that was it; I was going to bolt. Brother Stanley said, "I'll tell you what, brother Keith, let's go back downstairs and you can go back outside and smoke a couple of cigarettes. Then you will have to throw them away."

My Mom and Brother Stanley had to do some paper work and so my dad and the girl that I was seeing walked outside. Once outside, my dad said, "What do you think?"

I replied, "I can't believe this place. What's with all this Brother Keith and Brother Stanley Stuff?" They started laughing and I said, "Man, this going to be tuff!"

My dad said, "Your mom is pretty scared about the whereabouts of this place."

I looked at my dad and said, "Dad, I've been in places that would make a Billy Goat puke. It's okay."

He replied, 'I know. I think you should give it a try, besides I kinda like the whole Brother Keith stuff." We all had a good laugh again and went back inside. Brother Stanley said that I couldn't have any contact with my mom and dad for the next two weeks and I wouldn't get to see anybody for the next four months. I thought, *Man this is going to be really something*. Let's see here, no phone calls from anyone, but my parents and that was once a week for five minutes. There were no T.V's, no Newspapers, and no contact with the outside world. That was a lot to get a handle on when your body was going to start craving the crack and the heroin. My folks and the girl that I was staying with were taking driving away because as hard as I was, we all knew what was ahead for me. My brain wasn't exactly hitting on all cylinders. And soon enough, I was going to be in some pain. Teen Challenge doesn't give you Librium to detox with like the other rehabs had done. We all finally said our good-byes and they drove away.

Brother Stanley took me into his office and had me fill out some paperwork. Then, we went upstairs and he showed me where my bed was. He began to tell me what all the rules were, what time we had to be up, how long I had to get a shower, be dressed and down stairs ready for prayer. The rules just kept on coming, It was like a five minute shower. Again, I thought, *Oh My Gosh! What have I agreed to*. In a few minutes, some of the guys had come inside from working and he introduced them to me. These guys introduced themselves just Like Brother Stanley said they would. Hi my name is Brother Rob and my name is Brother Steve and so on. I really didn't know what to think about this place that was located right in the middle of the lower 9th ward. That night they let me sit in on their study group because the next day, I started my first day of class at Teen Challenge. We had dinner that evening and surprisingly the food was actually pretty good. I asked who the cook was and they said Brother Cliff. I said Brother Cliff? Is he a student? They replied yes. We have someone from the center who has to cook. That scared me because, I mean, I could cook some, but I wasn't the greatest cook. Afterwards, we had to go upstairs for study time.

This place was like Bible College. They started telling me that Brother Sampson, who was the Dean of students, was like a military drill sergeant. I laughed. The staff members let me skip the study time session because they didn't know what Brother Sampson would have me to do. So, I was allowed to take a shower and go to bed. That night I really wanted a smoke, but I made it through my first night and they cut the lights off at ten o'clock sharp. I actually had to share a room with twelve other guys. It was known as the twelve man room. I had never shared a room with so many guys and I had no idea of the snoring that I was going to have to endure for the next year.

The next morning at 6:00 sharp, the lights came on and it was as if I were in Vietnam. The guys were scrambling around like someone had just thrown a grenade under their bunks. I just laid there for a few minutes when one of the guys said, "Brother Keith, if I were you, I would get up and make your bed. You have fifteen minutes to have your teeth brushed, your face washed and be down stairs."

I asked, "And what happens if I don't?"

He said, "Brother Stanley is gonna give you a hook up."

I ask what a hook up was. He said, "That's when you don't follow the rules and the staff will give you a chore. Every time you get hooked up, the chores are worse.

I laughed and said, "What, are we in Jr high school?"

He shrugged and said, "Look man, sometimes they will hook us all up for one person's actions, so please don't take the chance of getting us all hooked up."

I remember thinking these guys are nice, but man they are soft. Which was definitely not the case. I got up, washed my face and brushed my teeth. We reported downstairs and everyone, without speaking, walked over and found a place to pray. They were actually taking cushions from off of the sofas and placing them under their knees to pray. One of the guys said, "Brother Keith, you need to find a place to pray. We pray silently every morning like this for fifteen minutes."

I said, "Huh?"

He replied, "Yeah brother, now go ahead and find you a place."

I thought, *You have got to be kidding me.* I had never prayed a day in my life except to ask God to help me in extreme instances in my life. I found a place, knelt down and spent the next fifteen minute wondering what we were having for breakfast. Afterwards, we gathered around in a circle and everyone held hands in order to bless the food. *Really? Hold hands? A bunch of guys, c'mon give me a break! Is this place for real?* As we were eating our breakfast, the staff member that was working was named Brother Pop's (Rip). He was, I suppose, in his late fifty's or early sixty's back then. At first, he came across as a grumpy old geezer. Even acted downright mean. That was just his outer shell. Brother Pop's was a man who had lived a very hard life. He actually had a heart of gold. You wouldn't know it when you first met him though. Brother Pop's had been incarcerated and spent time in Angola State Penitentiary on a couple of different occasions. I got to know Brother Pop's pretty well and I never knew why he did time, I never asked. Brother Pops had gone through the program a few years before and was asked to stay on as a staff member. Brother Pop's would give you your work schedule for the day. Right after breakfast, we had to clean the whole facility. One week you may be in the laundry room the next you could be in the kitchen or cleaning the bathrooms. There were plenty of chores you were going to do at Teen Challenge. Brother Pops would also tell you where you were going to have to work that afternoon.

Teen Challenge is supported in several different ways. When I went through Teen Challenge, there was a lawn care service, a car wash, snow cone stand, even a firewood business. People would sometimes donate money. From what I understand, these days there are other ways that they are earning money to support Teen Challenge. After we were through cleaning the center, Brother Pops approached me and said, "You and I have to take a ride."

I asked him, "Where we are going?"

And he replied, "It's none of your business, but if you just have to know, I'm taking you down to the welfare office."

I asked, "Why?"

He said, "You are going to be here for a year. Do you think we are just going to feed you for free? Look! This Ministry is self supported and it takes money to feed all of you knuckle heads. We are going to house you and feed you. It's not a lot, but it will help out."

Once we arrived at the welfare office, I had to go in and wait forever to be seen. I looked around the room and I felt disgusted, but not how you might think. I was disgusted with the people who were sitting there waiting for a hand out.

What was I doing in the midst of these slime balls? I felt like I was above these people. I was humiliated to say the least. What I didn't think about was the elderly people that really needed the welfare and food stamps to survive, or the people that were sitting there with blank looks on their faces because they had just lost their jobs and had no idea what or how they were going to survive. I'm sure that there were many other reasons why they were there as well. It was probably one of the most humbling experiences of my life.

After I applied for food stamps, Brother Pops drove me back to the center. We hardly spoke on the way back. I think he sensed I was feeling the humility of what had just incurred. Once we were back at the center, I was sent upstairs to the class room. I walked in and there sat all the guys. There were probably sixteen guys in the room at the time. I saw a large black man standing at the front of the room. No one had told me that Brother Sampson was black. And he was large and black. You see, Brother Sampson had gone through the program years ago. He was from Boston. He had also robbed people with his pit-bulldog in the city parks in and around the Boston area. He would actually walk up to people and tell them to give him their belongings and such or he would be forced to turn his dog loose on them. He was actually a pretty scary guy. But he had given his heart and life over to Jesus and was now employed at Teen Challenge as the Dean of Students. He looked at me and said, "I don't want you in the classroom today or tomorrow. I want you to stay in the twelve man room and do some paper work."

We drug a desk out of the classroom and down the hallway back to the twelve man room where we bunked. He asked me if I had a composition book. I said, "Yes sir, I do," and I was left alone to start writing a document of my drug history and my family history as well. As I settled down, I was amazed at how loud this guy's voice was. It almost sounded as if he was yelling the whole time. He would ask guys questions and if they didn't have an answer, he would let them have it. I remember, one of the guys didn't turn in his homework. Man, you would have thought it was the end of the world. He chewed on this guy for a solid ten minutes. I was thinking, *Dude, lighten up for crying out loud.* He told this guy that he might have forgotten it last night, but that he wouldn't forget it tonight. He told him, "Tonight, you will write 2 Corinthians 8:11 one hundred times before you go to bed. 2 Corinthians 8:11 says this, *Now finish the work, so that you eager willingness to do it will be matched by your completion of it, according to your means.* I thought, *You have got to be kidding me. This guy is out of his mind. This brother had to write all of this scripture after he had fin-ished all of his class work.* As I sat there listening to Brother Sampson, I could tell this guy really knew the Word of God. At noon, the class was over and we went downstairs for lunch. We gathered around, made a circle again, held hands and prayed. I quickly came to the conclusion that these guys prayed about everything.

After lunch, we were to start our jobs that we had been assigned to. I was on the carwash detail. Once we were out-side, we started washing cars. People from the neighbor-hood knew that we were out there daily. The cars would pull in and we had a guy who was in charge of the hose, about three guys actually washing the car, a couple working on the wheels and tires, and a few more would be drying. These people would pull up and would have their radios on. I was washing a car when this guy pulled up. He had 50 cent on his radio and the song "Go Shorty, It's Your Birthday" was playing. I started smiling and singing along with the radio. I looked up and Brother Sampson was standing there staring at me. He looked at me and said, "You are hooked up."

I said, "For what?"

He said, "This is a ministry and we conduct ourselves in accordance worthy of the Gospel of Jesus Christ."

Under my breath, I snickered and said, "Whatever dude."

He called me upstairs to the classroom and gave me my punishment. He told me that I would wash every dish, every pot and every pan. I can't prove this, but I know without a shadow of a doubt, that Brother Sampson went in and told Brother Cliff to dirty up every pot, pan, and skillet that he could muster up, because I have never seen so many dirty dishes. The way he handled it was even worse. Once we gathered around the dining hall that night, he told everyone to leave their dishes right where they were because Brother Keith was going to clean them. This included sweeping and mopping the floors in both the dining hall and the Kitchen. I didn't get through until 9:45 that night, which left me 15 minutes to get a shower and go to bed. I was really starting to hate this place.

The next morning, it was the same song and dance. I mean the same routines as the day before, except this time Brother Stanley approached me and said, "I need to see you Brother Keith."

I said, "Okay," and so he took me upstairs to my bunk.

He said, "Have a seat." I sat down and he said, "Tell me what happened yesterday out at the carwash."

I replied, "Brother Sampson is tyrant, he hooked me up and made me wash all the dishes last night."

He said, "Look! We are not going to put up with any foolishness here Brother Keith. You either get on board or we are going to need to call your folks to come and get you."

I just sat there for a minute with a blank stare on my face. I was thinking, *You have got to be kidding me*. Finally, I said, "Brother Stanley, I was just singing along with a song on the radio."

He said, "Brother Keith, we are known in this community for being followers of Jesus Christ. We are Ambassadors of Jesus, and we do not, and will not, promote the foolishness of secular music here at God's House. Brother Keith,

I want you to know right now that this is God's House and it's sacred. We are secluding you guys for a reason. You will understand all of this later. Now, I'm going to give you a scripture to memorize for tomorrow. It is out of the book of Proverbs Chapter 17:12 - *Better to meet a bear robbed of her cubs than a fool in his folly.* You need to have this turned in tomorrow before I get here."

I just stared at Brother Stanley. There was something I really liked about Brother Stanley, but at this moment, I was really pretty perturbed at him. I still didn't see the big deal of what I had done. I copped an attitude for the next few days. I wasn't really trying too hard to make any friends, either. I thought they were all a bunch of wackos. Brother Sampson, I guess, was trying to figure me out because he made me stay in the twelve man room for a few extra days and day after day, I could hear him in there preaching and teaching the Word. I still had a really bad attitude.

Finally Brother Greg Dill, who is the executive director of Teen Challenge, finally called me down to his office one day and said, "Brother Keith, have a seat. You have been here for 4 or five days now and you still seem to be having a hard time with the way we do things around here."

I asked him, "What do you mean Brother Greg?"

He said, "Look at your face! Look at the countenance of your face."

I replied, "What's wrong with my face?"

He said, "You have so much anger inside of you that it's pitiful. I also think that you are full of pride." He looked at me and said something that has always stayed with me. He said, "Some people will tell you that you need to swallow your pride. I'm telling you not to swallow your pride, and in fact you, need to spit your pride out because if you swallow it then it's just going to come back up at a later time."

That made sense to me. Then he asked me what I wanted. I said, "Honestly, Brother Greg. I think I just want to go home. I don't think this is the place for me."

He looked at me and asked, "And why is that?"

I answered, "I just want to quit the dope and I don't see how this place is going to help me."

He said, "is that how you really feel? You haven't even given this place a chance."

I said, "Brother Greg, what makes this rehab different from any of the others?"

He said, "Well, for one Brother Keith, this is not a rehab. Also you will, in the process, have a relationship with Jesus."

I replied, "Brother Greg, I don't care about a relationship with Jesus. I just want to quit doing dope."

He grabbed a dictionary out of his desk and turned quickly to the word rehabilitate. He plopped it down on the desk in front of me and said, "Read me back the definition of rehabilitate." It said something like this, to rehabilitate is to bring something or someone back to its former state of being. When I looked up at Brother Greg he said, "Why in the world would you want to be brought back to your former state? Your former state had you smoking crack and shooting dope."

For the first time in my adult life, it was as if a light bulb had just gone off in my head. Brother Greg said, "Keith, if you will honestly try and give it a chance here at Teen Challenge, there will be a renewing of the mind. You will also gain that relationship with the Lord. Keith, the Lord loves you and wants a relationship with you. But you are going to have to surrender to Him," and then he said, "Brother Keith, if you do so, I believe you will be surprised at how easy it will be to stop using drugs. You have already been here for four or five days and you haven't used. Keith, I believe in you."

That was a great talk. I could tell that Brother Greg was a really genuine man who really loved God. I felt a lot better when I left his office. I went back upstairs and took time to reflect on the talk that Brother Greg had just given me. That night, I had to write the scripture that Brother Stanley had given me. That night was really tuff. For the last night or two, I had started craving the drugs really bad. I remember having woke up in the middle of the night and walking over to one of the staff member's rooms, who was on duty to get fresh linen, to change my sheets because of the sweating. I started having to bite down on my belt at night from going through withdrawals from the heroin. I couldn't figure out if it was from the heroin or a combination of the heroin and crack together. I don't know. All I know is that it was horrible. When that would happen, the guys in my room, instead of getting mad, would ask me if I was okay. A few of the guys would even get up and ask me if I was okay. They would say, "Hang in there, Brother Keith. It's going to get better." I would hear those guys praying and asking God to help me.

At first, I was really angry because I didn't want them praying for me. I wanted them to leave me alone. I used to call them hypocrites. I remember saying to myself, "Listen to them. Those prayers aren't real. They are just praying out loud so they can listen to one another." Now, don't get me wrong. We were with each other twenty four hours a day. You could tell who was seeking God and the guys that had just got there. The one's seeking the Lord were not getting caught up in any foolishness. There were some guys that had come in right before me, and others had come in since I had first gotten there. We had some moments where tempers would flare. We had a room full of guys coming straight in off of the streets. We were all street smart, and had been in lots of tuff spots in our lives. We were all con artists, but we all had a couple of things in common, when we first walked through those doors at Teen Challenge. We were all lost and we were all used to running game on everyone we came in contact with. The Beautiful thing about Teen Challenge is you aren't running game on anybody there. Those staff members had seen it all.

Brother Sampson finally let me join the classroom. I had been listening to him teach the class; now I was finally going to get to listen to him up close. Brother Sampson was a man of God for sure and could teach the Word of God like crazy. I didn't like him at all when I first got there. I thought he was going to be the reason I left for sure. Brother Sampson was hard on every one of us. Looking back at it, he had to be. We were a bunch of thugs when we first got there. There are two phases at Teen Challenge. The first 4 months that you are there is called the Induction phase. It's like a Christian boot camp. The primary goal is to get the Word of God in you while at the same time you are coming off of the drugs. At least, that's how I perceived it. The second phase is actually up in Winnfield, Louisiana. Brother Gary Bentley and his wife are the directors there. That is where the guys who are truly seeking God go, if they make that far into the program.

While I was there, I watched so many guys come into the program and then leave, that I couldn't even keep count of all of them. It's really sad because some guys would come in and stay for a few days and get some rest and three hot meals then leave and go back out and hit the streets. It's what they called three hot's and a cot, just a place to find rest. There were at least two guys, that I remember, who left the center and within a couple of weeks were dead. My mom and dad had given me a brand new Bible a few years back, but I had never even opened it. Well, I was getting ready to put it to use.

There was a scripture that Brother Sampson used to quote to us every day, 2 Corinthians 5:17, *Therefore if any man be in Christ, he is a new creation; the old is gone, the new has come.* I heard Brother Sampson quote that verse every day, but this day was the first day that it had registered as to what that scripture actually meant. I started really listening to the Word that he preached. I didn't realize it at the time, but what was happening was God's Word was beginning to come alive inside of me. The guys were still wanting to pray for me, and with me, but I wouldn't let them. There was a part of me that was not wanting to surrender to the Lord. I remember hearing Brother Sampson saying, "The Steps Of A Righteous Man Are Ordered By God." He said that scripture every day.

The days rolled on and He kept teaching and preaching, and I could actually feel my heart start feeling sort of funny. My stomach would begin to knot up when he would start preaching. I went into Teen Challenge around the last week of February 2003 , and on the morning of March 10th 2003, we were sitting in the class room and Brother Sampson was teaching class. Brother Sampson looked out at us and said, "You know, some of you guys are going to come to a cross-road in your lives where you are eventually going to have to make a decision whether or not you are going to continue down the path you have been on. In Jeremiah 6:16, this is what the Lord says, *Stand at the crossroads and look, ask for the ancient paths, ask where the way is, and walk in it, and you will find rest for you souls.* A path that will be better; a path that will be more productive and help you restore everything that Satan has stolen from you." And then he recited John 10:10, *"The devil comes only to kill, steal, and destroy; Jesus comes so that you may have life, and have it to the full."* Then Brother Sampson said, "I know you guys have lost people in your lives because of your addictions: wives, kids, jobs. How much more are you guys willing to lose? Your lives and your souls? What shall it profit a man to gain the whole world just to lose his soul? The Bible says that *God will restore all that the locust and canker worm hath devoured from you.* Guys, that is a promise from our God. He will restore it all, not some of it, but all of it. Now I have to run up town for a few minutes and so you guys can turn the stereo on and play some praise and worship music and pray. You guys utilize this time wisely or I'm going to hook you all up."

One of the guys put on a Michael W Smith CD. The music was playing softly and I could hear these Brothers praying. And I heard a couple of them praying for me. Only this time, I wasn't mad at them. I could hear how sincere their prayers were. I started thinking about the words Brother Sampson had said in class, about the crossroads and how the devil had robbed me of everything. What was happening to me? I started to tremble and all of a sudden, I felt like I was going to start crying. I had not really cried since Greg died. I didn't want to cry in front of these guys. I wasn't going to do it. And then this song came on. It was called Let it Rain. In this song, he is singing about the Holy Spirit Raining down on us. I was thinking about how I had really never even given Jesus a chance in my life. I was seeing my children's faces. The girls I didn't get the chance to raise. Kade, who was just a little boy and was sad that his dad had just abandoned him. A wife that I really loved more than life itself. And two of the best parents that ever lived, they had dealt with the pain of losing their youngest child. And instead of being a son that should have been a good son, I had become a dread to everyone. I broke down. I hadn't cried in years. I cried out loud to God. "Please Lord, forgive me. Please come into my heart and change my life God." And then these guys that had been praying for me for weeks ran over to me and cried with me. I kept crying and crying. I couldn't stop. The funny thing was it felt good. I remember just asking the Lord to please forgive me and take my life that it was His and I wanted to be a changed person. I kept thanking Him over and over. For the first time in years, I felt clean. I was feeling like a human being. I said, "Lord, I have never ever talked to you like this. Lord, you are saying that you will give me strength? Well, if I'm going to do this your way, then I'm asking you to take away these cravings I'm having for the drugs. Lord, I can't do this on my own. And Lord, if you can, I am really wanting a cigarette too, so take that burden too, if you don't mind."

I guess it was another thirty minutes for all of us in there rejoicing and laughing and smiling. I can't speak for any of the other classes, but the class that I went through in Teen Challenge; they were a great bunch of guys. I remember the rest of that day, I had a big ole stupid grin on my face, and what was crazy was I would just start crying at the drop of a hat. I had never had this feeling before. If you remember, in the first of the book when I mentioned the part about the lightning bugs and the smell of the summer rains, I knew that I now was going to have my life back. That night, as I was lying in bed, I started praying and telling Jesus how thankful I was to be his child and how good that felt. I was asking Him to forgive me for the time I had committed this sin and that sin. I suppose I was thinking about all the horrible things that I had done in the past and I asked the Lord how He could forgive me for everything that I had done. I remember saying, "Lord, how is it possible that You could forgive me for all of it? Lord, I was so bad, and caused so many people so much pain."

It was then that I heard in an audible voice that sounded like He was whispering into my ear. He said, "My Child, I love you more than you will ever know. I love you so much that I will go to any length to reach you. I even used your drug dealer to get my Word to you, one day." And it hit me! The Gideon's Bible that the drug dealer had given me that night. I started bawling and hit my knees again. I started crying uncontrollably. I haven't stopped crying since. That night, when I finally went to sleep, I had the most sound, deep sleep that I had had in years. And when I awoke the next morning, the sheets were dry. I didn't feel the cravings for the dope. I didn't want a cigarette. I couldn't believe what I was feeling. I had been healed of the cravings of the drugs and nicotine. And just like that, the cravings stopped. There is no doubt in my mind that the Lord knows our hearts, because the second I made up my mind to stop using, that was it, the cravings stopped. That is how powerful our God is. People say in these days and times that God doesn't perform miracles in today's world. That's one of the biggest lies that there is. I can tell you right now that I was in Teen Challenge with a bunch of miracles.

In the following weeks, I started growing in the Lord. There was hunger coming from within me. I know that besides having a relationship with Jesus, Teen Challenge has been the most instrumental tool in my life. The tool God used to corral me. They say one year in Teen Challenge is the equivalent of seven years of Sunday school. Studies also show that only 12% of secular programs are successful in people overcoming drugs. 86% of people that go through Teen Challenge go on to live productive lives and stay off of drugs. I knew nothing about the Lord when I went into the program. The teaching was incredible. Many times, I heard Brother Greg, Brother Gary, and Brother Stanley say this will be the best year of your life. You are in a Jesus green house. Just you and Jesus. I couldn't get enough scripture in me. At Teen Challenge, you have to learn two scriptures a week. At first I was like, Man this is way too much to try and remember. Now I know why they do. When you have the Word of God written on the Tablets of your heart, you are a lot less prone to struggle. Hosea 4:6 says, *My people are destroyed for lack of knowledge.*

I remember the first time I got hooked up in the bathroom at Teen Challenge. Lights went off at ten o'clock. I got up out of bed and slipped into the bathroom and was reading the Bible. The door opened up and it was one of the staff members. He said, "Brother Keith, what are you doing in here?"

I said, "Reading."

He saw that is was the Bible and said, "Well, you know the rules, you're hooked up."

I said, "Yeah, I know."

He shut the door and walked out. He opened up the door a few seconds later and had a smile on his face. He said, "You know, we hate to hook you guys up, but in this case it's a good hook up."

I asked, "Can you tell me what my hook up is?"

He said, "Yeah, give me Romans 13:1-2 50 times. *Everyone shall submit himself to the governing authorities, for there is no authority except that which God has established. The authorities that have been established by God. Consequently he who rebels against the authority is rebelling against what God has instituted, and those who do so shall bring judgment on themselves.* I can't tell you how many times I had to write that scripture while I was in Teen Challenge. It wasn't the last time I was hooked up for reading the Word in the bathroom at night. Nor was I the only one getting hooked up for that reason. It seemed like every night someone was getting hooked up for getting caught in the bathroom reading the Bible.

What Brother Greg had told me about there being a renewing of the mind was starting to happen right before my very eyes. I could not believe how clearly I had begun to see things. I wasn't mad at anyone any more. And all that anger that I had kept pent up from the depths of my soul seemed to be gone. I walked around with a smile on my face. I even saw that old tyrant Brother Sampson in a different light. Now don't get me wrong, he didn't have any problem still hooking a brother up. And I know that if he was hooking you up, it was out of love and he just wanted the best for us. One day in class he told us that we were going to be tested in Teen Challenge to see where we stand in our relationship as we grew in the Lord. And test they did. One morning, I got dressed and went through the morning ritual of getting dressed and putting all of my personal belongings in order. If you have one piece of clothing lying on your bed, or if one of your shoes were sticking out from under your bed too far, then you were going to get a hook up. I finished my tiding up and went downstairs to pray and eat breakfast. Brother Stanley came into work and got his morning coffee as he always did. He, then, would proceed upstairs to check out the twelve man room. After a few minutes, he came downstairs and announced, in front of everyone, that Brother Keith was hooked up. I was furious. I asked him what I was hooked up for? He said my bunk was a mess.

I said, "That's a bunch of crap."

He said, "What did you just say?"

I said, "There is no way my bunk is out of order. In fact, Brother Stanley, I have the cleanest bunk in the whole twelve man room."

I got a few ugly looks from my Brothers when I said that. Brother Stanley said, "Well, I guess you are calling me a liar then."

I replied, "I'm not calling you a liar, Brother Stanley I'm just telling you that I know for a fact that my bunk was clean when I came downstairs."

He said, "Come with me upstairs."

Once we were upstairs, I could not believe what I saw. There was a shirt lying across my bed, my shoes were pulled out from under my bunk and were strewn out in the middle of the floor. I began ranting and shouting like a possessed person, like I had a demon who had just taken up residency inside of me. He let me rant and scream. I even threw in a couple of expletives. He finally said, "Are you done?"

I answered, "No sir, I'm not done. It had to have been one of the guys that has done this to me Brother Stanley!"

He said, "Brother Keith, I'm really disappointed in you my brother."

I asked him, "Why are you disappointed in me?"

He replied, "Brother Keith, I messed up you stuff."

I said, "WHAT?"

He explained, "I wanted to see where you are at in your walk with the Lord." I stood there with what had to have been the most retarded look ever on my face. He went on, "Brother, if you get this mad out there in the real world, then the first time you get mad out in the world, you are going to fall flat on your face."

I felt like a failure. I was wanting to please God so bad, but in an instance and out of anger, I lost control of my temper. He hooked me up and told me it was a double hook up. The first scripture he gave me was for cursing. Ephesians 4:29 *Do not let any unwholesome talk come out of your mouths, only what is helpful for building up others according to their needs, that it will benefit those who listen.* And the second one was for my temper tantrum. It was also in Ephesians 4:26-27 *In your anger do not sin Do not let the sun go down while you are still angry. And do not give the devil a foot hold.* He had me write those fifty times a piece. After you write those scriptures down that many times, they become imbedded in your brain. They become part of you. And that is one of the benefits of the power that is in the awesome Word of God, because once God's Word is written on the tablets of your heart, you can defend yourself when the enemy attacks you. You have your sword and shield that you can extinguish the fiery arrows that Satan shoots at you. In the sixth chapter of Ephesians, it talks about the warfare of the spirit-filled believer. Because our fight is not against flesh and blood, but against the rulers, against the authorities, against the powers of the dark world and against the spiritual forces of evil in the heavenly realms. Therefore, we must put on the full armor of the Lord so when the day of evil comes, we will be able to take our stand against the devil's schemes. (Ephesians 6:11-12) It is very important as new Christians to build a foundation, so that we can stand up against all the sin that Satan is going to try and ensnare us with.

The Bible says, *Be self-controlled and alert, your enemy the devil prowls around like a roaring lion seeking whom he can devour.* 1 Peter 5:8. The reason those two guys died when the left the center after only a few days is this, they had no foundation to stand on. Luke 6:49 *But the one who hears my words and does not put them into practice is like a man who built his house on the ground without a foundation. The moment the torrent struck the house, it collapsed and its destruction was complete.* I was really enjoying the relationship that I was having with the Lord.

The weeks passed by and I was able to speak to my parents every week for five minutes. There were a few stretches where I was hooked up and my privileges were revoked. Brother Sampson and I butted heads a few more times. He was always victorious though. He said that like the apostle Paul had a thorn in his flesh, I was the thorn in his flesh. Brother Sampson said something one day that really got my attention. He said, "You brother. The Lord has blessed me with a gift of discernment. And what he has revealed to me about you is that you have run over everybody that you have ever come into contact with. Here is a news flash for you. I got your number buddy. You aren't going to run over me."

I took that several different ways. For one, here was a very large black man who was kinda scary and I really didn't want to push him too far. And two, I knew he was a man of God and by this time, I had read enough of the Bible to see what happened to people who messed with God's anointed. Brother Sampson and Brother Stanley kept me hooked up so much that I didn't have time to keep up any foolishness. Teen Challenge is about Jesus 24 hours a day 7 days a week. One Saturday night we were lying in our bunks getting ready to go to bed. I suppose it was around eleven o'clock or so. There were a couple of bars on the same block as Teen challenge. On Saturday nights, it would get really crazy outside of the center. Franklin Avenue had a boulevard running down the center of the street with pretty plush green grass growing in the middle of it. The patrons, who were visiting the clubs, would set up bar-b-que pits in the middle of the boulevard on the grass and cook. It would go on until the wee hours of the morning. We were lying in the bunks and all of a sudden, a gun fire rang out. The shooting started and didn't stop. It continued for what seemed to be like an eternity. We all started falling out of our bunks. It sounded like someone had broken into the center and was killing everyone in the building. I was the first to crawl over to the window and peer down to see what was going on. What we saw sent chills through our bodies. People were running and screaming. People were crawling under vehicles. Suddenly, the shooting stopped. Right below us, on the sidewalk, the body of a kid about eighteen or nineteen years old was lying there. He was moaning. He had begun to cry. We could tell he was not going to make it. We looked out into the middle of the street and there were bodies lying everywhere. We watched this kid take his last breath right before us. We sat there in dead silence. I remember thinking that I had just watched this kid enter into his eternal destiny. We moved away from the window and gathered by the door in our room. We sat there holding hands praying for these kids who had just lost their lives here on this earth. As we were praying, Brother Sampson burst through the doors and found us sitting in a circle praying. He gave us a look of relief to see that we were all okay.

He said, "Are you guys okay?"

We said, "Yes."

He said, "You guys keep praying and lift their families up in prayer."

He went outside and stayed for a really long time. When he came back in, he told us that 5 young men had died in the middle of the streets outside of the center and that it was a gang related shooting over a girl. As we crawled back into our bunks, I remember lying there thinking how blessed I was that I didn't perish in my sin. No one knows what was going through this kid's mind as he gasped for his last breath. I have always hoped, in my heart that, with his last breath, he cried out to the Lord and asked Him to forgive him for his sins. The Bible says we should be prepared in season and out of season. None of us know when or how we will leave this earth. I thank God for His mercy and His grace every day. After that, I had a different outlook on life.

Brother Stanley and I had become extremely close. Every now and then, he would gather up a couple of guys that had been really digging in and seeking God. One Saturday, he took a few of us to hit golf balls at a driving range. That was a huge blessing. Brother Stanley is someone that I still seek Godly counsel from. He, Brother Greg and Brother Gary, I can call these guys anytime day or night and they will give me advice in any situation that I am facing. Men of God! We all need Godly men in our lives. Men that will keep us accountable to God, and to one another.

Brother Stanley approached me one day and said, "Brother Keith, I need to talk to you."

I replied, "Okay."

He said, "I have been on the phone with a judge up in Ruston. You have a court date tomorrow."

I asked if it was about a fight that I had gotten into a year or so before I came into Teen Challenge.

He said, "I tried to get the judge to let us postpone the date for a few months, but he refused. He said that they were upgrading your charges from simple battery to aggravated battery due to the nature of his injuries. If convicted, you will have to do some time."

I said, "I understand Brother Stanley." I was pretty shaken up about it. I asked him if he thought I should pack my bags and take all my clothes with us.

He turned around and said, "Let me tell you something. That judge up there isn't the high judge Brother. Let me quote a verse out of the Bible to you. Philippians 1:6, *Being confident of this very thing, that he who has begun a good work in you will carry it to completion, until the day of Christ Jesus.*" He looked at me, smiled this huge grin, and said in his Italian voice, "Brother, that judge is getting ready to see who the real judge is." He winked at me and put my mind at ease.

When it comes to the Lord, Brother Stanley never counts out the Lord in any circumstance. I honestly think he actually speaks things into existence. On the ride up there, we had a great time talking about the Lord the whole way. As we approached Ruston, he said, "Against my better judgment, I'm going to do something that I wouldn't usually do. After court, I'm going to take you by your house and let you see your mom and dad. We don't do this for a reason. People have left the program because they see their people and get home sick and within a day or two they walk right out of the center and out of the will of God. You are far enough along in your walk that we think you will be okay."

I sat there smiling. I was going to get to see my mom and dad. Maybe this trip would turn out okay. I still don't have any idea what happened when we went to court. They called my name and I went up in front of the judge. He looked down at his paperwork for a few seconds then he looked up and said, "So, you are in Teen challenge in New Orleans."

I replied, "Yes sir."

He asked me how long I was going to be there and I said about 8 more months.

He said, "Were you court ordered to be there?"

I answered, "No sir."

He said, "You went there on your own?"

"Yes sir."

He asked me how long I had been there? I said, "Almost four months."

He looked at the prosecutors and said, "I am going to make a motion that we move this until after he gets out of Teen Challenge."

And just like that, it was done. Brother Stanley was smiling when I turned around. We got in the car and Brother Stanley said, "Do you remember that scripture?"

I asked, "Do you mean Philippians 1:6?"

He smiled and said, "That a boy."

We drove over to my mom and dad's house. As we pulled into the drive way, I saw the door swing open and Kade came running out towards the car. My son was six years old. I fought back the tears as hard as I could. I didn't want him to start crying. He ran and jumped into my arms. For the first time in my life, I felt like a daddy. I wasn't bound by any chains. I had been set free. Galatians 5:1 *It is for freedom that Christ has set us free, Stand Firm ,then, and do not let yourselves be burdened again by a yoke of slavery.* Kade and I held each other and smothered each other in hugs and kisses. My mom and dad came over to me and hugged my neck. My mom didn't try to hold back the tears; she let them roll. But they were tears of joy. My dad had a look of peace on his face that I had not seen in years. I had gained all of my weight back, plus a few pounds. We didn't get to visit, but a few minutes Brother Stanley knew it was going to be hard enough for us to say our goodbyes. We were standing in the driveway and Kade was playing with a basketball.

I said, "Hey little buddy, daddy's got to go."

He dropped his ball, walked over to me and said, "I thought you were going to stay."

I said, "I have to go buddy, but I'll get to see you again real soon." That was the hardest thing I ever went through.

My Mom had to pry him off of my legs. He would not turn loose of my legs. I told him I was a lot better, but that I had to do this and that we would never have to be away from each other again. He didn't care; he was hysterical. It was a pain that ripped me to the core. It felt as if my insides were being shredded to pieces. For the first time in many years, I could feel things again. For years, my heart was so calloused. Now, my heart was so tender. I was finding out, for the first time, that when Jesus gets a hold of your heart, it is the greatest feeling in the world.

I pray every day that I will be sensitive to the Holy Spirit. Once I got inside of the car and we backed out, I looked at Brother Stanley and he was as broken down as I was. I don't know who was crying the hardest, me or him. He said, "Brother, I have never witnessed anything like that in my life. I know you are going to be fine."

I said, "Why do you say that Brother Stanley?"

He said, "Brother, if you were able to get in this car and drive away with that beautiful little boy hanging on to your legs like that, I know you are truly seeking the Lord."

Things got really quite for a little while on the ride back to New Orleans. We had a nice peaceful ride back. Within a few days of getting back, Brother Greg came up to me and said, "We have the date of your graduation." It was three Saturdays away. He said, "You can invite your whole family to come down for it. We will have a party with ice cream and cake and that sort of thing."

I was so happy because I knew that I was growing spiritually and I knew that they thought I was ready to move into a deeper walk with the Lord. That felt really good. I knew that my mom and dad would see to it that my girls would be there. I couldn't wait to see them. I know I was always a good daddy in a certain way. I just was never around them, and also I was very dysfunctional. I knew I wanted Kade there, too! I just didn't think Leanne would have any part of it. She had been really hurt and told me repeatedly how much she hated me. So I was not thinking that she would ever let him come with my parents to New Orleans to see me graduate first phase. I wrote her and told her that I had found the Lord and that I was sorry for the misery I had caused her. I told her that I had been praying that the Lord would soften her heart, so that she at least wouldn't hate me for future purposes. We had been divorced for a little over a year at this point and I told her that I knew these words were probably going in one ear and out of the other. I told her that if she could just think about it, I would appreciate it. I knew it would probably be a week or so before I would have an answer.

That night, I was lying in my bed when there was a knock on the door. It was one of the staff members. At this time, I was no longer residing in the twelve man room. Your last month or so you stay in what is called the four man room. It's where guys, who are getting ready graduate from the first phase, stay before departing for North Louisiana. The Staff member said, "Hey, you guys want to come to my room for popcorn and a root beer float. But, it's BYOB."

We started laughing and one of the guys said, "Yeah bring your own Bible."

We were out of our bunks so fast. At Teen Challenge, I learned to be very grateful for the little things in life. As humans, we take for granted every day the things that the Lord provides us with. Things like hearing and seeing, touching, and the sense of smell. We all go through life not really counting our blessings. As we went into the staff members room, I thought how awesome is this. It's Saturday night and I'm sitting in the lower ninth ward in New Orleans, Louisiana getting ready to eat popcorn and drink a root beer float. Talk about a change in lifestyles. I thought back to a time when on a Saturday night it was pretty much a sure bet that I was going to be getting high. As we sat there, we had the windows open with a fan blowing gently on us. It was just like that scripture I had learned 4 months earlier. 2 Corinthians 5:17 *Therefore if any man be in Christ he is a new creation, the old has gone and the new has come.* I knew, in my heart, I was a new creature. It felt so good to have feelings again. My memory was coming back to me. I was able to remember things about my childhood. And that made me happy.

As we sat talking about our upcoming graduation, Brother Hammer asked all four of us if we had given any thought about what our plans were when we were out of Teen Challenge. None of us had a clue. All we knew was that Jesus would let us know when we got to that place. Then he asked us if we had ever thought about what heaven was going to be like? I sat there for a minute and thought. I said, "Brother Hammer, I don't think I can even get a small idea of what it will be like."

He said, "1 Corinthians 2:9 says, *No eye has seen, no ear has heard, no mind has conceived what God has prepared for those who love him,* but God has revealed it to us through His Spirit. The Spirit searches all the deep things of God. What do you think it will be like?"

We all looked at each other and smiled. One of the guys said, "I don't know Brother Hammer. You tell us what you think it s gonna be like."

Brother Hammer started to smile and said, "Well, I think that when we get there, we are going to see sights that are so pleasing to the eyes, and these beautiful colors that we have never seen before. The air will be so fresh with fragrances that you have never smelled before. I think the Lord will have made a place for us that it's going to completely blow us away."

Man, Brother Hammer had us thinking like crazy. I said, "Hey, you never know Brother Hammer, I would love to see rainbow colored raindrops."

The guys laughed and said, "Man, you done seen too many skittles commercials, Brother Keith."

One of the guys said, "Man, I bet everything is going to be in like 3D." We were just sitting there hanging out. I have never had a root beer float that tasted as good as that one did. It got quiet for a minute and then Brother Hammer said, "You know, right now the Lord is sitting on His throne. And he is loving this."

We all looked at each other like what's he talking about? We all thought Brother Hammer had gone on and checked out on us for a minute. I said, "What do you mean Brother Hammer?"

He said, "Yep, the Lord is probably talking to his angels right now saying to them, Shhhh ,shhhh, listen to those guys down there on Franklin Avenue," he said, "You know, God Loves it when we talk about Him like this. He is probably telling the angels right now that you can see Me and you love Me, but see, my children down there on Franklin Avenue have never seen Me before, and yet, they are down there talking about Me and saying how much they love Me. And that makes Me happy."

You know when he said that, there was a peace that came over me that was incredible. I know the other guys felt the same way, too. We went back to our rooms and got some sleep because we had to be ready for Church the next morning. Sundays were always good. Sometimes we traveled on Sundays and would share our testimonies at different churches around south Louisiana. That good ole peaceful feeling didn't last long because Brother Sampson came in on Monday morning ready to hook up everybody in the house. And he did hook me up that day twice. In fact, I think he hooked me up every day until I left for Mount Grace.

Mount Grace is in Dodson, Louisiana. That is where you go for the second phase of Teen Challenge. As we were getting ready to go north, we all started trying to find out if

Brother Gary was going to be as tuff as Brother Sampson was. I guess every class is different because we heard all kinds of stuff about how Brother Gary would have you cut and stack a cord of wood at night by yourself if you got hooked up.

I received a letter from Leanne that week and I was shocked at what I was reading. Not only was she going to allow Kade to come, but she asked if it would be okay if she came to the graduation. I was so excited at the thought of having everyone that I loved coming down and meeting all of my brothers and seeing where I gave my life to Jesus. I had no idea how powerful prayer was. I mean, I had asked God to take the taste of drugs away from me and He did. I asked Him to let me stop craving cigarettes and they stopped. I prayed that the judge would show me some mercy and grace and he did. And I asked the Lord to soften Leanne's heart so she wouldn't hate me, and it looks as if she doesn't. Man, God is good. I did find myself, that week, feeling kind of sad. I knew that I would never be back in the classroom as a student. These men of God had poured so much into me and all my brothers that it was a very bittersweet time before I left. I knew that I was leaving the first phase with a whole lot of scripture written on the tablets of my heart. I was truly amazed at how much of God's Word is put on your heart while you are in Teen Challenge.

All week long, Brother Sampson tried to see where I was at in my walk; he poked and prodded on me a good bit. I never wavered because I knew that I may have had to spend an extra six months in the program if I made him mad. On the night before my graduation, I was so nervous that I couldn't sleep a wink. Brother Greg and Brother Stanley called me into the office the next morning and they told me that I was getting ready to go into a deeper walk with the Lord. They said that in the second phase Brother Gary would teach in depth and I remember thinking, *My gosh I have probably learned more from Brother Sampson in the last four months than most people learn in a life time.* I didn't mean that in a conceited or grandiose way at all. How much more in depth could it get? That is just how intense that the teaching is in the Teen Challenge program.

Brother Greg always had a kind word for the students at Teen Challenge. He said, "Okay, you Mighty Man of God. You know what to do, now go do it. Brother Keith, whatever you do in your walk with the Lord from this day forward, you must do these two things. You must daily read your Bible and pray daily, as well.

I said, "I understand Brother Greg."

I was really nervous about seeing everyone for the first time in a while. It would be good to see them. Brother Stanley had even told me that I could ride with my folks up to Mount Grace. I was going to have at least six hours to catch up with the folks. My folks showed up about 10:00 o'clock.The girls looked like they had grown a foot since I had seen them last. Kade was his usual hyper self. My mom looked really pretty in the dress she was wearing. She looked a little fidgety. She was okay, though. My Dad was a rock. Lefty was always calm, cool, and collected. And then, Leanne came in. She was as beautiful as ever. She was very nice to me. She hugged my neck and said, "You look great! You have gained a bunch of weight."

I said, "Thank you! And you, as well, look great."

I will admit that my heart was racing just a little bit. I introduced my family to all the guys in the program and all the staff members. At graduation, they invite people from area churches, other friends and acquaintances to come and attend the festive occasion. There was an older lady who sang at the church we attended on Sundays. It was Brother Greg's home church. This lady used to sing for Jimmy Swaggert on T.V. The guys, who were graduating, could ask whomever they wanted to sing for their service. And so, I asked Mrs.

Minnie to sing "Midnight-Cry". I had heard her sing that song a couple of months earlier and she had me in tears. She wouldn't disappoint on this occasion either. Every person in the building was crying except for Kade. He just wanted to eat! The graduates had to stand up and say a few words about their time at Teen Challenge. We were able to express our heartfelt gratitude towards the Staff. And I also told my Brothers that I loved them and would see them shortly. Graduation was always sad for the guys left behind. They knew they would see the guys again up at Mount Grace, but you had gotten so used to praying with these guys. Some of them were there when you came to Christ. They cried with you, they saw you when you were struggling trying to come off of the drugs. They were your Brothers. And there was a special bond between you and these guys. I thought that I had been through a lot until I got to Teen Challenge. We had all been through a bunch of stuff. A lot of these guys were just products of their environment. So many people were raised by parents who were drug addicts as well. Some had alcoholics for parents. Others came from abusive homes and broken homes. One brother, who grew up in the lower ninth ward, told me that on some nights they would be riding in their car. There might be two in the front and two in the back of the car when a gunshot would go off from inside of the car. He said he would look in the back seat and the shooter would take the guys dope that he had just shot and open up the car door, shove the guy out of the car onto the street and they would keep driving. I had heard a lot of these stories like this one.

We could see the miracles that God was performing right here in this day and time. We were in Sunday school class one Sunday morning and some older gentleman said that he wished God would still perform the miracles that He used to back in the time Jesus walked the earth. One of my brothers stood up and said, "Excuse me sir, but if I may interrupt you for a second sir. You are looking at fifteen miracles sitting in the same room with you right here.

We all started clapping our hands and gave our brother a standing ovation. Every person in that class stood up and clapped with us. The older man was very sincere and gracious. He apologized and said, "You guys are so right. You are miracles of God."

I think that God performs miracles every day. We just miss seeing them. I also think that the Lord would be defeating His own purpose if He were still having to perform the miracles He did back when He walked the earth. At some point, faith had to enter in. We have to just live this beautiful life that He has given us. The Bible says that He knew us before we were ever even knitted together into our mothers' wombs. I think our spirits did know Him before, and maybe He said, "You guys are going to leave Me for a little while, but you will find your way back to Me." That's why it is so important for us to persevere in this short lifetime. And that is just so awesome to me.

As we all finished speaking, Brother Greg spoke and told stories on each and every one of us. I remember a couple of the things Brother Greg said about me on that day. He said that when I came through the doors of Teen Challenge, I was one of the most mule headed guys he had known to come through the doors at the center. He said that, for sure, I was the most prideful person to come through. He said, "I wasn't too worried though, because I knew he had to go through Brother Sampson's class." And everyone laughed. He said, "But look at him now."

Brother Stanley would take a photo of you on the day you came into the program. Brother Greg held up that photo. He said, "Look at his eyes. No Hope! No Love! No Future! It is really amazing to see what God will do in our lives if we will only surrender to Him and allow the Holy Spirit to work in our lives."

We all hugged each other and Brother Sampson walked up to me and said, "Hey knuckle head." I turned around he gave me a hug and said, "You got this!"

I said, "I got this Brother Sampson."

He said, "I love you brother!"

I responded, "I love you to Brother Sampson."

He was extremely tuff on me. I am glad he was. It was the hardest to say goodbye to Brother Stanley, we had become really close. I think everyone really loved Brother Stanley because he was a truly genuine man. He would get so excited about the Lord. He cried with all of us on many occasions. He was like a brother, a friend, the Man of God, and a whole lot more to each and every one of us. We walked out to the vehicles and my mom said, "Keith, why don't you ride with Leanne and your dad and I will take the kids with us."

I looked at Leanne and was stunned at first, she nodded yes. I said, "Okay, great let's go."

I got into the car with Leanne and we laughed, talked and she said, "Wow. I can't believe how good you look."

I said, "Well, that's the joy of the Lord I suppose."

I still couldn't believe I was riding in the car with the person I loved more than anything in the world. That is, besides the Lord Jesus Christ. She wanted to know everything there was to know about Teen Challenge. I told her many of the things that went on. Things that I didn't have room enough in this book to share. I think she was truly amazed at the amount of scripture that was hidden on the tablets of my heart. She looked at me and said, "Keith, I really didn't think that you were going to stay at Teen Challenge. Every week, I would think that I was going to get a call from someone and they were going to say 'I saw Keith in town,' the call never came."

We stopped and had lunch with my family. We had the chance to just relax for a little while. It felt really weird not being at the center. We caught up on what was going on in our hometown. After lunch, we got back in the vehicles and proceeded on our way to Mount Grace. We listened to the radio; the ride was almost electric. After a little while, Leanne turned the radio down and said, "I need to talk to you."

I said, "Okay, what's up?"

She said, "Keith, I have been seeing someone." It kind of caught me off guard. She said, "He treats me really good. I'm really happy for the first time in a long time."

I knew who the guy was; I was kind of shocked and stunned. I didn't know what to say or how to react. I remember thinking, *Lord, you need to give me strength to process this and handle this in the right way.* She knew I was stunned because I had become very quite.

She said, "Keith, I loved you more than life itself, but you severed our relationship and our marriage when you chose the drugs over our family. You seem to be changed and I really think that you are. And if you ever loved me at all, then I hope you will just be happy for me." And boom! when she said that, I thought, *Man, she is right.* I had every chance in the world to bring her all the happiness in the world that she deserved. She picked up my hand and said, "Are you okay?"

I smiled and said, "Yeah, I'm ok."

She said, "Since you are doing so well and you guys pray so much, will you pray for my relationship?"

I sat there for a minute thinking, *Wow! This is kinda a weird feeling. The woman I love more than anything is asking me to pray for her and her boy friend.* I thought to myself. *We are divorced, and I was living with someone when I went into Teen Challenge. I made her life a living hell.* I looked at her and said, "Sure Leanne, I'll pray for you guys."

She smiled and said, "Thank you."

Within a few minutes, we arrived at Mount Grace. We got out and my family and I met Brother Gary and the staff members there. They showed us where my cabin was and we were given a tour of Mount Grace. It was beautiful up there. There was the most beautiful Chapel you have ever seen sitting on the very center of the property. It was surrounded by a bunch of cabins that we lived in. There was a huge dining hall that also served as the classrooms. After the tour, I hugged all of my kids and Leanne. I gave my Mom and Dad a big hug and they said, "We will see you next Sunday."

I said okay and watched them drive away. Well, things looked as though they had just changed a great deal in the lives of the people that I loved. I realized that I may have been away in a place that was secluded from the outside world, but people had lives and they were going on with theirs. I knew, in my heart, that Leanne had given her all in our marriage, and I knew, as a new person in Christ, that I had more important things that needed to be done right now. Seeking God with all of my heart was the number one priority in my life at this time. 2 Chronicles 7:14 *If my people who are called by name, will humble themselves and pray and seek my face and turn from their wicked ways, then will I hear from heaven and will forgive their sin and heal their land.* I knew that the most important thing that I could do was to humble myself seek and His face. That was a promise I would do, if He would heal my heart and deliver me from my addictions. And so, I put everything else out of my mind.

Brother Gary was nothing like Brother Sampson. He was kind of quiet, but there was a seriousness about Brother Gary that you felt really comfortable with talking to him on any level. I had seen a picture of Brother Gary in New Orleans. I think it was a mug shot of him from a prior arrest. He looked like a triple axe murderer. I was surprised when I got to Mount Grace and he looked nothing like the mug shot.

I settled in at Mount Grace and absolutely loved it up there. Mount Grace had a thriving firewood business going on there in North Louisiana. I remember the first time I saw the "Sea Of Firewood". I just stood there staring at row after row of these waves of firewood. I saw a splitter and I felt better. I quickly learned that the splitter was only used by one or two people a day. I was new up at Mount Grace and so I was a rookie. It was now June and it was the middle of the summer and it was HOT! If you got hooked up, you did time on the wood pile. You had to split a rick of wood, which is a half of a cord. And that is still a lot of firewood after you have already split firewood all evening for about 4 and a half hours. I remember all of the guys being down at the firewood pile and somebody would quote a random scripture. For the next hour, all you could hear would be me and my brothers shouting out the Word of God coming from out of that sea of wood. I have never had such solid, deep sleep in my life.

Mount Grace was nothing like the first phase of Teen Challenge. Up at Mount Grace, you had the liberty to go in and out of the chapel as you pleased. There was a stereo system in the chapel and you could go in there and listen to praise and worship, read the Word of God, and pray. We spent many late nights in the chapel. I learned, at Mount Grace, that, sometimes, when you wake up in the middle of the night and can't sleep that one of two things are happening. Either the Lord is wanting to talk to you, or He is waiting to hear from you. I had no idea that God sometimes wants you to be still and listen for Him. Those are some of the most peaceful times, I think, we can have is when we are still waiting to hear from the Lord. The difference in the first and second phases of Teen Challenge is that Brother Sampson was showing us how to achieve Salvation, and Brother Gary was teaching us how to basically live the life of a Christian. It was like going from the book of acts in New Orleans, to the epistles and the general epistles at Mount Grace. The teaching at Mount Grace was awesome.

Brother Gary's wife, up at Mount Grace, was an incredible woman of God as well. She ran the Mount Grace thrift shop a few miles away from Mount Grace. The months rolled by rather quickly. My mom and dad would follow us around from church to church every Sunday as we went and sang for different churches and shared out testimonies as well. Each Sunday, my mom and dad would be at the church when we arrived. They were so happy. I could see it in their faces. They could finally see a change in their son.

One night, I was lying in my bed when I was suddenly awakened out of a deep sleep. A thought had come to my mind. I put my clothes on and ran to the chapel. Once inside the chapel, I walked up to the alter and knelt down at the foot of this big, beautiful cross that was placed in the middle of the alter. I began to pray. I realized what was wrong. For the last couple of months, I had prayed that the Lord would bless the relationship that Leanne was in. The Holy Spirit within me had apparently been grieving because it was, all at once, letting me know that the guy she was seeing might not even be a Christian. And what if he wasn't? What if he was never going to have my wife and son in church? What if they would never know Jesus? I changed my prayers from that night on. For the rest of the time I was at Teen Challenge, I prayed that if, and only if, that man had my wife and son in church then, and only then, would I pray that the Lord would bless that relationship. I believe that is why we need to be so sensitive to the Holy Spirit. Because being led by the Holy Spirit is the greatest gift given to us by God.

I went on my way in Teen Challenge growing spiritually every day. My roommates at Mount Grace were awesome. One was a Cajun whose name was Matthew Powell. He was only about 5'6". The other was a huge guy about 6'5" and 330 lbs. His name was Steve Kaled. We called him "Big Steve". Big Steve was probably hooked up more than anybody who had ever come though the Louisiana "Teen Challenge". This Brother was covered with demonic tattoos. He has since gotten them taken off. Me and those two guys had an unbelievable bond. You love all your brothers while you are there. But with others like these two, we became more like biological brothers. We had a bond that would always keep us in touch with each other. Matthew and I have been able to stay in closer contact with each other, and see each other a lot. He has a story that is unbelievable. There were young guys that went through the program with me who had been given juvenile life, but if they would go through, and complete, the program, it would cut time off of their sentence. It was an amazing thing to watch guys come into the program and see the power of the Living God go to work in these guy's lives.

I remember Brother Gary having all of us sing I Can Only Imagine in the Teen Challenge Choir. That song had just come out. I remember the first time I heard that song, I cried like a new born baby. We were singing that song in the choir every time we went to a different church because it was so powerful. I can honestly say that I don't think that I ever made it through that entire song without completely breaking down. One Sunday morning, I looked up when we were singing that song and I saw my mom standing in the back of the church with her hands raised and she was crying like a baby. I will never forget what she looked like standing there with her hands raised worshiping the Lord.

After Teen Challenge, I went back home to Ruston. I knew my first order of business was to find a good Church. I had some of my buddies who had been asking me to come to their church. It was a really good church with a really sweet Spirit. I was hoping that my mom and dad would accept Christ and come to church with me. They did and loved the Church. There was a guy named Brad Martin leading the music when we got there. I knew him and used to see him staggering out the local pubs in town. He was a good bit younger than me. I was surprised to see him leading the music for sure. I remember the first Sunday we went to the church; I asked the Lord if this was where He wanted me to be, then to give me a sign. As we entered the church, I stopped at the door and I heard the song that the choir was singing. It was "Let it Rain", the same song that was playing in the classroom the morning I gave my life to Jesus. When I told Brad that he said, "Keith, are you kidding me?"

I said, "No, why?"

He replied, "We had never sang that song in church before. In fact it was a last minute decision."

I felt the presence of the Lord in the church that morning. The next week, my dad was saved and my mom was saved the week after that. The pastor of the church could preach an unbelievable sermon. I didn't have a job and didn't know what I was going to do. I didn't even have a driver's license at the time. Brad had just gotten laid off of his job at the plant he was working at and so he was washing houses. Brad and I became the best of friends. I was coming out of Teen Challenge and I was used to having all these guys with me and we were spurring one another on in the Bible. Now, I was back home staying with my folks and would just sit at the house, read the Bible and pray. Brad would pick me up every day and let me work with him. God really knows what He is doing because Brad was a walking Bible. I had no idea he knew the Bible like he did. We went back and forth over and over the scriptures every day. God had put Brad in my life to be there at a time in my life that was crucial. It could have turned out completely different had he not been there when he was.

My old friends were calling the house to see if it was true that I had become a Jesus freak. There is a verse in the Bible that says *Bad company corrupts good character*. I didn't need those old friends because the Lord wanted to be there for me. Brad didn't really need any help washing those houses. And I'm sure it took money away from his bill money and food money to feed his wife and two boys. I was sitting at the house one day when the phone rang. My mom said, "Leanne is on the phone and wants to talk to you."

I said, "Okay," and answered the phone. She was asking me about the church. She asked, "What denomination is that church you are going to?"

I said, "Well Leanne, it's not a denominational church."

Leanne was raised in a very staunch Methodist Church. She said, "Well, is it one of those spirit filled churches."

I knew where she was going with this so I said, "Yes, it is." I decided that I would have a little fun with her.

She said, "I don't know if I want our son going to one of THOSE churches."

I responded, "Well, I don't really know what you mean by one of THOSE churches."

She said, "Aw c'mon Keith, you know what I'm talking about."

I said, "Leanne, if you are talking about one of those churches where people love Jesus and want to live their lives for Christ and want to have the liberty to raise their hands and praise God and worship him freely, then yes, I am attending one of THOSE churches. Leanne, let me say this. I lived with you for 6 years and in that 6 years I never watched you so much as crack open a Bible. So you need to be careful when you are sitting there judging people on how they want to worship the Lord. If you want sit in church quietly and worship the Lord, then that's your prerogative. But when you see Jesus standing there in all of His splendor, did you ever stop to think that there just might be a little shouting and singing going on?"

She got really quite and said, "I'm sorry. I had no right to say that."

I asked, "What brought all of this on anyway?"

She answered, "Kade came home after he went to church with you and he said it was the most fun he had ever had at church. He said everyone was singing really loud and shouting and it just concerned me."

I said, "Okay. Leanne, don't worry about anything. Kade will be just fine in the house of the Lord."

She replied, "Okay. Well, I feel better now." Then she asked if I wanted to stop by the house the next day and get Kade and take him to mom and dad's house for a few hours. I said that would be fine. The next day, Brad and I worked all day and I asked him if we could stop by and pick Kade up and he said sure. We pulled in at Leanne's house and we went up to the door. When she opened the door, Kade ran and jumped into my arms.

I said, "Leanne, this is Brad."

They talked for a minute and finally I said, "Well, we better be going before your boy friend comes over."

She said, "It's okay. He won't be here for another 30 minutes."

When we drove off, Brad said, "That was the weirdest thing that I have ever witnessed."

I asked, "What do you mean?"

He answered, "Keith! That is who you are supposed to be with."

I started laughing. I said, "Brad, I had my chance with her, but I killed that relationship a long time ago brother."

He said, "Man, that was really weird."

He took us over to my mom's house and dropped us off. The weeks rolled on and I just kept digging into the Word and enjoying my walk with the Lord. Church was awesome and life was good. One evening, there was a knock on the door. It was Leanne. My mom told her to come on in and she came into the den where I was sitting, reading the Bible.

She said, "Is that all you do is sit here and read the Bible?"

I answered, "Well Leanne, what do you suppose that I should do?"

She said, "Your truck is sitting right there. You should get out of the house and go do something."

I explained, "I don't have a driver's license. If I go and get in that truck and take off, I know that I will get pulled over and arrested. Everyone in this town will be saying, 'I knew he wasn't a changed person.' And in doing so, I will hurt the Lord, Leanne, and that's not a chance that I am willing to take." She understood. I asked her, "Where is Kade?"

She said, "Oh, he is still at school."

I responded, "Oh, okay."

She asked, "Can I talk to you for a minute?"

I answered, "Sure."

She said, "Not in here. Can we step outside?"

We walked outside and she said, "I need your advice."

I asked, "About what?"

She explained, "I'm not so sure that me and this guy that I have been seeing are supposed to be together. He is a really nice guy, but things just aren't working out."

I said, "Really. I'm really sorry to hear that Leanne."

About that time, her phone rang and she turned around to answer it. As she turned around, I gave a Tiger Woods fist pump, looked up towards heaven, and under my breath said, "YES! Thank you Lord!"

After she hung up the phone, she said, "What do you think I should do?"

I said, "Leanne, you know I can't get involved in that decision. That will have to between you and the Lord."

She said, "I figured you would say that."

I said, "Just go to the Lord with it and search your heart."

She replied, "Okay, well I better be going. I will see you later."

I went back in the house and sat there in shock at what I had just heard her say. My mom came in the room and said, "What did Leanne want?"

I answered, "Aw nothing, she just wanted to talk."

The next morning, Brad came and picked me up and I told him what had happened.

He said, "I knew it. I already told you that she is the woman that you are supposed to be with crazy. I'm telling you that the Lord is going to put you guys back together."

I said, "Hang on Brad. I don't want to get ahead of myself."

He laughed and said, "You just wait and see. Keith, that woman still loves you man. I could tell it the first time I met her. I saw it in her eyes, the way she looked at you."

I said, "Brad Martin, you are as crazy as a run over dog."

We both laughed and went on to work. That afternoon, he dropped me off at the house and again I was sitting in the den when there was a knock at the door. My mom said, "Keith, its Leanne."

I walked to the door and she motioned for me to come outside. I walked outside and she smiled and said, "I did it."

I asked, "You did what?"

She answered, "I broke up with him."

I didn't know how to act. I said the first thing that popped out of my mouth, and it was, "Aw Leanne, I'm sorry to hear that." I remember thinking, *Lord, please forgive me for that lie I just told. Sorry to hear it. That was music to my ears.*

Then she said something that just completely blew my mind. She said, "Look, I have to run over to Monroe this evening to pick Kade up a Cub Scout uniform. Would you like to ride over there with us?"

I said, "With you and Kade?"

She said, "Yes."

I replied, "Sure Leanne. I would love that."

She said, "Great. Kade is going to be really excited. Okay, I will be back over here in an hour or so to pick you up."

I said, "Great. I'll see you then," and she drove away. I remember standing in the garage for a few minutes and I thinking about the day I got saved in Teen Challenge. I remembered that verse in the book of 2 Chronicles 7:14, *If my people who are called by my name, will humble themselves and seek my face and turn from their wicked ways, then will I hear from heaven and will forgive their sins and heal their land.* God was doing more for me than I ever thought possible.

I walked into my parent's house and my mom said, "What are you doing?"

I answered, "I have a date in a few minutes. I'm going to Monroe."

She asked, "Who is your date with?"

I said, "Leanne."

My mom's face went pale. She said, "What?"

I said, "Yeah, she asked me to ride over to Monroe with her to get Kade a Cub Scout uniform."

When I turned around to see the look on her face, she was gone. She had run out into the back yard where my dad was at, and was telling him the news. She was elated. I went ahead and jumped in the shower. I got dressed and stepped into the kitchen where my dad was standing there pouring himself a glass of sweet tea. In Louisiana, it's sweet tea because that's how we roll down here. He sat his tea down and walked over to me. He hugged my neck and said, "I love you son."

I said, "I love you too, Dad!"

He said, "God is good, isn't He?"

I said, "24/7 Pops."

Leanne drove up in the driveway and my heart was pounding so hard I thought it was going to explode. I got into the car and looked in the back seat. Kade was grinning like a mule eating briars. He said, "Dad, I'm a Cub Scout."

I replied, "I heard."

That little fellow asked me nine thousand questions on the way to Monroe. Man, it felt great being a daddy. Once we were in Monroe, we went to a store and picked up his uniform. Leanne said, "Let's eat Mexican food at El-Chico's in the mall. I'm buying."

I said, "Leanne, I have money."

She said, "I know, but tonight's my treat."

My pride was creeping back in and I remembered what Brother Greg had said about my pride. I didn't say another word. We pulled into the mall and went inside. We were strolling through the mall and Kade ran in between us and started holding our hands. We walked along looking at each other and smiling when Kade did the unexpected. He put my and Leanne's hands into each others, then jumped directly in front of us and started walking backwards watching Leanne and I hold hands. He had a huge smile on his face and said, "Now, that's what I like." Now we were all grinning like a bunch of mules eating briars. We went into the restaurant and had dinner. Then we drove back to Ruston. Kade had fallen asleep on the back seat and that gave Leanne and I time to talk.

She said, "You know, I think we should maybe start to see each other if that's okay with you."

I said, "Uh, okay by me!"

She replied, "I think it would be good for Kade's sake."

I said, "Oh, most definitely. You know, Kade really needs both us in his life."

She said, "Oh yeah. I couldn't agree more. So, tell me about this church you guys are going to."

I responded, "It's awesome, Leanne. You can feel the presence of God when you go into the church and the people really love the Lord."

She asked, "Do you think I could maybe go with you guys this coming Sunday? But now, I don't think I know about all that shouting and raising the hands and all that stuff, so if you don't mind, we should probably sit in the back of the church."

I laughed and said, "That will be fine."

The next Sunday, we walked into the Church and I walked straight down the middle aisle right down to the second row. I turned and looked at her, and she said, "I'm going to kill you."

I said, "Good, then I'll be walking with Jesus before it gets dark this evening."

She smiled and when the church service began, I looked over at her and she had the most peaceful look on her face. After Church, we went back to my mom and dad's house where we ate lunch. She said, "That is the first time in my life that I didn't want church to end."

My mom said, "I know, isn't it awesome."

Two weeks later, she was saved and was immediately baptized. In less than a two month period, my mom, dad, and Leanne had come to know the Lord and had been baptized. I was in complete awe of what the Lord had done in my life since I let Him into my life. How could He do all of this that fast? Ephesians 3:20 *Now to him who is able to do immeasurably more than all we ask or imagine, according to his power that is at work within us.*

Mount Grace Teen Challenge
Keith

We were re-married on a Sunday night right before church. I had invited a bunch of my friends that didn't know the Lord in hopes that they might find Him. We were a happy family again except this time; we had the Lord in our lives. Brad Martin and I had become best friends and we spent endless hours in the Word of God. I continued to grow spiritually every day. We loved our church and we loved our church family. Life was good.

One morning, I woke up and Leanne was standing beside the bed looking down at me smiling. I asked, "What in the world are you grinning at?"

She said, "You are getting ready to be a poppa again."

I know I must have sounded like Scooby Doo because the first thing out of my mouth was, "Huh? ruh row! Are you sure?"

She said, "Yep." I asked her if she was ok with it. She smiled and said, "We are going to pray for a beautiful baby girl."

I started smiling and said, "Well then. The Mitchell family is going to be a whole brighter in a few months."

Brad picked me up that morning and he said, "I have some good news."

I said, "Me too. You tell me first."

He said, "We have to go meet a guy at the huddle house about a job. It's in the oilfield. It's going to be right down the road in Vernon, Louisiana. I'm going to try and get on and soon after, I'm going to get you hired on."

I smiled and said, "Right on."

He asked, "What's your good news?"

I answered, "I'm getting ready to be a daddy again, buddy."

He busted out laughing and said, "You crazy thang. Who do you think you are, Father Abraham?"

I said, "I recon so Brad!"

He hugged my neck and we went and met this friend of ours about this job. It went down just how we hoped it would. Brad got the job and started making great money. There was a guy who went to church with us named Jerry Hunter. He had a lawn care service. He knew that I had been working with Brad and knew that he had just gone to work in the oil field. He approached me after church on Sunday morning said, "Hey brother Keith, you looking for a job?"

I said, "Heck yeah."

He said, "You can run a crew on my Lawn care business for me."

I said, "Awesome."

He said, "There is one stipulation, though."

I said, "Okay, what's the stipulation?"

He answered, "Every week, I go to the Parish Detention Center and teach a Bible class. I think you would be perfect for it."

I said, "Okay."

I had no idea how rewarding that was going to be. I know that God blessed me so much through ministering to these guys. The inmates knew that I had been there. I even knew some of them from "East End". A few of them were like, "Man, I remember you. You're that white boy that was over there in the projects more than most brothers were." We would laugh and they couldn't believe the change in my life. Some of them would say, "Brother, you don't even look like the same guy."

I would tell them, "That's because I'm not!"

I worked for Jerry for several months. One day, Brad called me and said, "Keith!" I could tell in his voice that he was excited. He said, "Meet me out at our office right now. My boss wants to meet you."

I went out there and met with the guy. He was a huge guy who came across as a real ruff guy. He asked me why I wanted to go to work in the oil field.

I said, "Well, I have a baby on the way and I want to better myself for my family."

He said, "You aren't going to ask for time off all the time."

I said, "No sir."

He said, "You ain't going to complain all the time are you? Cause I got enough of those kind."

I replied, "No sir, not gonna do that neither."

He said, "Be here in the morning."

I am positive of this, when you are in the will of God doing the things you are supposed to be doing, God will bless you. He can't help Himself. He loves us that much. I went home and told Leanne. She was seeing firsthand the blessings of God. He said that we would be blessed in the city and blessed in the country; blessed coming in and blessed going out. We were in church every Sunday and every Wednesday. Leanne was getting ready to have the baby. Leanne's grandmother was very sick in the hospital. She would ask every day, "Is that baby here yet?"

My mother in law, whose name is Beck, would say, "No mother, she's not here yet."

Finally, on May 2 2005, Mary-Micah Mitchell was born. She was so beautiful. She came into the world screaming and she is still, to this day, screaming just as loud and just as much. But I wouldn't trade one second of it. She is the little bundle of joy that the Lord has so richly blessed us with.

Beck went back to see Leanne's grandmother right after Leanne had the baby. She said, "Momma, Leanne had the baby. It's a big, beautiful, baby girl. They named the baby after you."

Her name was Mary-Alice Harmon. Beck told her that Leanne and the baby were both doing great. She died shortly after hearing that. We were amazed that she hung on until she knew that Leanne and the baby were going to be fine.

Later in the week, my mom was in a car wreck. She was rushed to the hospital, they took some X-rays of her lungs because she told them her ribs were hurting. They didn't find any broken ribs, but what they did find was spots on her lungs. My dad came to me and told me the news. They ran tests and told us it wasn't cancer, but it was just as bad. It was Pulmonary Fibrosis. Immediately, the church was praying for my mom. I couldn't believe this was happening now. My mom had been through so much, this couldn't be happening now. We were all in church together having a great life. My mom had become very sick very fast. She was miserable because she had a new grandbaby and wasn't getting to spend any time with Mary-Micah. We do have a few pictures of Mom holding Mary-Micah. It was devastating to our whole family. My mom and dad had been married for 44 years. They had both been retired for just a couple of years. I am so glad that I was living for the Lord at this time. My mom was able to have peace in her life knowing that I was serving the Lord Jesus Christ.

Mom was in a lot of pain. The doctors actually put her into a coma. She was in for about two weeks. While she was in a coma, they had to put a tracheotomy in her throat. We knew that when she came out of the coma and found out she couldn't speak to us, it was going to be really sad. We cried and cried. My mom was a Christian for only a couple of years before she died. But for those two years, she was seeking the Lord with every fiber of her being. She had the heart of a servant.

One day, I was sitting in her room with my dad. I was looking at her face and I began to weep uncontrollably. I had to leave the room and my dad came out into the hallway to check on me. He asked, "Are you ok?"

I said, "Dad, I just want the chance to tell her how sorry I am for causing you and her so much misery. I want to ask her to forgive me."

He replied, "Keith, she has forgiven you a thousand times over for that son."

I said, "Dad, I still want the chance."

He said, "Maybe she will come around."

We had our doubts. It was so hard for the kids to come in and see their Mimi like that. She loved her grandkids more than anything in the world. The kids were really hurting. One day, I had gone to the cafeteria to get some lunch. When I came back down to my mom's room, my dad met me in the hallway; he had a huge smile on his face. I knew she had come out of the coma. I went in to see her. She knew she had the tracheotomy. She was very weak. I knew this was not the time to have the talk with her. I was just so glad that she had come out of the coma. She actually started to feel better for about a week. She seemed to be getting stronger.

My mom had worked at the hospital and there were always people coming to see her. My mom was truly a wonderful person and everyone at the hospital would tell me that they hated to see her like that because she was so full of life. She was lying in the bed, one day, and she looked at all of us as we gathered around her bed and she mouthed to us that she was ready to go home. My dad said, "Don't worry momma, we are going to get you out of here real soon. We are going home."

She looked at my dad and pointed to the sky and mouthed again, "I'm ready to home." She kept pointing to the ceiling. We knew then she was ready to go home.

When I left out of there that night, I was in terrible shape. The next day, I was sitting in the room with her and dad. I looked over at her and she was staring at me. She smiled and mouthed the words "I love you." I got up and walked over to her bedside. My dad had been watching and he stood up, nodded at me and walked out of the room. I picked up her hand and held it.

I said, "Mom, I have so much on my heart I want to say to you. Mom, I want you to know that I am so sorry for all the heartache that I caused you and dad." She looked at me and tried to mouth something to me. I said, "Mom, I have to get this off of my chest." She smiled and nodded ok. I said, "Mom, Greg and I both know that we had the most wonderful parents in the world. I am so sorry that you have had to deal with so much heartache in your life. It's not fair. I am sorry that, on top of all of the hurt that you have had, you are going through this now. Mom, if I had just known what life was really all about. Having the Lord in our lives has been so awesome." I started to cry. "Being in church with you, dad and my family has been the best time of my life."

As she was lying there, I could actually feel my heart breaking. She had big tears in her eyes. She grabbed her note pad and started writing. It took her a few minutes to write what she had to say. When she handed me the pad, she handed it to me with a sweet smile. It said, "Keith, I have never been happier in my life. I know that I am on really short time. I don't want you having these feelings. The reason that I know what I do about the Bible is because you took the time to explain God's Word to me. Keith, your daddy and I despised crack cocaine. We hated it with all of our hearts, but the very thing we despised, eventually, ran you into the arms of Jesus. And because it ran you into the arms of Jesus, we ran into His arms following you. Keith, I love you with all my heart. The only thing I am sad about is that Mary- Micah will never know me."

I completely broke down on her bed. I told her that I would make sure that Mary-Micah knew who her Mimi was. I am so glad that the Lord allowed me that last conversation with my mom. You know, I have a lot of friends on face book. I post scripture on my wall sometimes 2 and 3 times a day. I'm sure that people think that I'm a Jesus freak. And that's okay because I am. I know that if you have read this book, then you can see how awesome our Lord and Savior is. I lived most of this book in complete darkness. And the other half, in his beautiful light. The Lord Jesus Christ has never failed me. My Mother passed away in the second week of October. It was so hard on us. My mom was the sweetest lady, and the best mom in the world.

THE BACKSLIDE

A fter Mom died, going to church was different. On Sunday mornings, it always seemed a little depressing and blue. I know that it wasn't because the Lord wasn't there. I suppose everyone feels that way when they lose a loved one. Especially, someone that was really close to them. It just takes time to learn how to adjust. Dad had been with my mom for almost half of a century, so he was completely lost.

My Mom

We would go over to his house and he would be sitting in his living room by himself in the quiet, just staring at the floor. As soon as we would start talking to him, he would break down. It was hard to see my pop in the shape he was in. Dad was always there for me. Even when a lot of people would have given up hope on their kid, my dad was always there for me. I really struggled to find the words to try and comfort him, but what can you say to someone who has lost the person that they had spent the better part of their life with.

When my Mom passed away, it was really tough on everyone. The difference between losing Mom and losing Greg is that we have a relationship with Jesus. I am so glad that we were all serving the Lord when my mom passed away. Outside of Christ, we are all in a very dangerous place. Had I not been serving the Lord when my mom passed away, there is a really good chance that I would probably be dead of an overdose right now. As it was, I went about my business going to church and serving the Lord, working in the oil field and spending quality time with my family. Mary-Micah was a blessing from above and she was so beautiful and full of life. Dad finally started to come around and eventually we would see him smile again. My son Kade was a big part the healing process for my dad. Kade and my dad were always playing. Kade had a way of making my dad smile. They have always had a really special bond with one another.

One day, my dad pulls up at my house and comes inside. He sits down and asks what I was up to? I could tell he had something on his mind, but he felt that he needed to make some small talk first and so I played along. After a few minutes, he said, "Son, I need to ask you something."

I replied, "Okay dad, what's wrong?"

He responded, "Nothing is wrong. I just wondered if you might think it was okay if I went out to eat dinner with a lady and then go to a movie."

I sat there completely blown away that my dad would ask my permission if he could go to dinner with someone. I know that it was out of respect for me, but still, I was just completely blown away. I looked at my dad and said, "Pop, you don't need to ask me if you can go to dinner with anyone. You were a great husband to my mom. You have always been a great dad to Greg and me both. I know that you may feel the need to ask what I think about the idea of you seeing someone else, but the fact is Dad, mom has passed away and she is not coming back."

He smiled and I could tell that he was glad that I wasn't uptight or going to be freaked out about it. The Lady that Dad was going to dinner with was the wife of one of Dad's best friends. He had passed away just 3 months before my mom did. They were both getting used to being widowers and I don't think either one of them was to keen on spending night after night alone. They started seeing each other and they really enjoyed one another's company. The relationship was really good for both of them. Her name was Kathy she was a really sweet lady. I had known her for years. It wasn't too long before they had set a wedding date to be married. Dad finally was getting back to his old self again. Kathy approached me one day before they got married. We were at my house.

Dad was playing in the yard with Kade and she said, "Keith, I want you to know that I loved your mom. She was an incredible lady. I just want you to know that I really love your dad and I would never try, nor could I ever take, your mother's place."

I could tell that she was very sincere. That spoke volumes to me about the character of this woman who was soon to be my new stepmother. My dad was finally happy again and I knew that he made her happy, too. I didn't really know her daughters very well at first. I'm sure that they had heard all of the horror stories about me and so, we kind of kept our distances at first. We have just recently begun to get closer to each other and all three are very sweet girls. Just the other day I thought, *Wow! I have 3 sisters. Right on!*

After a while, Dad and Kathy were married. I was my dad's best man. It was a very small wedding out in the country. They were very happy and so they started their new lives together.

One day, I got a phone call from my boss. He asked me what I thought about me moving over to the Dallas/Fort Worth area. I said I'd have to ask my wife. I told him that I would have to get back with him on that. We hung up and I immediately thought, *Lord, there is no way that this girl, who grew up in the country on Lake Claiborne, is moving to the big city.*

A couple of days went by and finally I said, "Hey honey, I got a phone call from my boss and he asked if I wanted to come to work over in Dallas."

She sat there for a few minutes and replied, "You are kidding, right?"

I said, "Yeah, I know. Don't worry, I told him you would never go for it."

She said, "WHAT? Are you kidding me? What did you tell him?"

I replied, "I told him that I would have to talk to you about it."

To my astonishment her face lit up like the fireworks on the 4th of July. She asked, "How much money?"

I answered, "A little bit more than I'm making now."

She spent the next week on the internet looking for jobs in the area. She is a registered nurse and so, a job for her was going to be a cake walk. I accepted the job and we moved over to Fort Worth. I didn't have a clue where anything was when we moved over there and so I stayed lost a lot. I buried myself in my work and was on the road a lot.

After a couple of weeks of getting settled in, we started looking for a new church home. None of the churches we went to felt like home. I think we were trying to compare the churches to our home church back in Louisiana. The one thing that I did know was that I had to find a church that was preaching the truth. The weeks went by and we kept trying to find a church home. As time went by I started making excuses about going to church. I was starting to meet people from different companies. Lots of weekends, I would take customers to play golf on not only Saturdays, but Sundays as well. After 5 years of seeking the Lord, I was starting to do the very thing that I was taught would put me in a dangerous place. I had started not reading my Bible daily. It would be a hit or miss thing as far as daily reading my Bible or hitting my knees to pray. We have to do these things daily to have an effective walk with Christ. We have to turn our ears to heaven daily to hear the plans that God has for us. It is like the relationship we have with our spouse or our children. We have to communicate daily with the Lord in order to have that special relationship that Jesus so desires to have with us.

In the past, I was a pro at tuning my wife out when she would want to talk to me about finances or if she was upset at one of our kids. I think it's called selective hearing. That is the same thing we do when we chose not to hear from the Lord. I had started allowing my flesh to stand directly in front of the Holy Spirit keeping my mind and my heart from feeling the tug from above. That is such a scary place to allow yourself to get to. Leanne would try and get me to go to church, but I always had an excuse. I didn't graduate from college, so the very fact that I was making 6 figures was mind boggling to me to say the least. What I didn't really realize at the time was that all of these things that I had begun to acquire, the nice home, the money, the good life that I now had were simply blessings from the Lord. And not, that I was just such an amazing sales person that everything was falling right in my lap. Believe me, when I tell you I had, once again, started to become a very self diluted and very self absorbed individual. I remember thinking, *Man, look at me! I am opening accounts that no one else in my company could open, I am the man.* What I was, was a guy who was in a very dangerous place.

One night, I received a phone call from a customer. He said, "Hey Keith, I need your help."

I said, "Sure, what's the problem?"

He replied, "A couple of my best hands are over at a strip club and they have run up a pretty large tab. Could you run over there and take care of it?"

Right then, I made a compromise. I should have made a stand, but I didn't. I went and paid their tab. That would be the first of many times that I would be expected to do so.

One day, after a round of golf, my boss asked the customers that we were playing with to go to a sports bar for a round of cocktails. They ordered mixed drinks and I ordered a coke. After a couple of minutes, they excused themselves to go to the restroom. Once they were out of sight, my boss said, "C'mon man, what are you doing?"

I asked, "What do you mean?"

He said, "Hey man, you need to lighten up and drink a beer with these guy's. They are corporate! You aren't in Ruston anymore. You are in the big leagues now."

Looking back, I realize how stupid he sounded when he said that. Like Brother Stanley told me one time, if you don't stand for something, you will fall for anything. After that, I would have a beer on the golf course. I started drinking at dinners and company functions. Pretty soon, I was promoted to Sales Manager. I was on top of the world. I had now completely taken my eyes off of the Lord. One day, I was driving down the road and I was changing radio stations when I heard a Christian song on the radio. I couldn't listen to it because I was so convicted. I quickly changed the station. As soon as I changed the station, a scripture came to mind. Mark 8:36, *For what shall it profit a man to gain the whole world just to forfeit his soul.* I knew the Word of God and yet, I had allowed sin to enter into my life again. Paul talks about the strife of two natures in the book of Romans in the 7th Chapter. He says in the 14th verse that, *We know that the law is spiritual; but I am unspiritual, sold as a slave to sin. I do not understand what I do. For what I want to do I do not do, but what I hate I do.* You see, I knew that what I was doing was wrong in the eyes of the Lord, but still I continued on living the life of sin. Satan had been sitting and waiting patiently for me to take my eyes off of the Lord. Just because we are born again does not mean that the father of all lies gives up on us. He has the rest of our lives to wait for us to become weak in an area of our lives that he knows he will be able to attack us in. That is why we must be prepared and girded up in prayer and in God's awesome and powerful Word. Remember, the devil is like a roaring lion seeking whom he can devour. I was on a one way street, headed the wrong way, doing a hundred miles per hour in a 20/mph speed zone. It was just a matter of time until the wheels would come off again.

There are a lot of men of God in the Oil and Gas business. A lot of them, I know, will not make the compromises that I did. I was as backslid as I could possibly be. I had a company man that wanted me to pick him up an eight ball of cocaine. We were doing a lot of business with his company and he gave me an ultimatum. Get it for him or find some other work. I told him no 3 times and eventually went and picked it up for him. I was scared to death when I picked up the eight ball of cocaine for him. An eight ball is three and a half grams of the stuff. I had to drive it from Fort Worth to Shreveport, Louisiana. I was scared to death. Once I got there, he asked me if I had the stuff then he said, "Let's take a ride to the next location that you guys will be working on and I will show you where I want you to put your equipment."

As we got in his truck, he asked me if the cocaine that I picked up for him was any good. I said, "How should I know? I don't mess with the stuff anymore."

He pulled off of the location and drove over to the other location that we were going to be working on. He showed me where to spot my equipment. Afterwards, we walked back over to his truck and left there to go back to my truck. We never made it to my truck. He pulled over on a dirt road back in the woods and stopped the truck. I asked him what he was doing.

He said, "I'm going to see if this stuff is any good." He pulled it out and drew out a couple of huge lines of coke.

I asked, "Don't you think those are some pretty big lines there brother?"

He replied, "Not really. One for me and one for you."

I said, "I'm not doing one."

He responded, "Come on man, one line is not going to kill you bro."

I said, "Look man, you don't know my past."

Bottom line was he didn't care about my past. He went on, "How do I know you are not going to call human resources or something?"

I said, "Man, that's the stupidest thing I have ever heard."

Finally, I gave in. You know the rest of the story. I started using daily. Within a few months, Leanne packed up her stuff and was gone. I had taken my eyes off of the Lord. When Leanne left this time, I thought, *Well, you have really done it this time*. The one thing Leanne told me the day she remarried me was that if I ever went back to drugs, she would be gone for good.

The Bible says that if we go back to our old ways, it will be seven times worse than we were before. I knew I was in deep trouble, but still I couldn't stop. I really thought I would die in my sin this time. The old man started to rise up in me again. I started to get angry again. This time, the anger was completely directed at myself. I had shut myself out from everyone. My oldest daughter, Lindsey, had moved up to Fort Worth about a year before and she could tell that I was in deep trouble. The last thing in the world that I wanted was for any of my children to see was me in the shape that I was in. She was devastated.

Lindsey called her sister, who was starting her freshman year at the University of Houston, and told her she was afraid for me and that I was in really bad shape. Logann called me and she was very upset. She cried, "Dad, are you okay?"

I lied to her and told her I was fine and for her not to worry, but inside I knew I was in trouble. For the next few months, I became a recluse. I started smoking crack again and Brother Stanley even called one night to talk to me. I was so ashamed that I wouldn't answer the phone. I was overwhelmed with guilt and conviction. In my mind, I was struggling with right and wrong, Ephesians 6 took on a whole new meaning, I knew that there was a battle going on in the heavenly realms, a battle over my soul. I could feel it happening. The Bible says that our fight is not against flesh and blood, but against the rulers and powers of the dark world. The Devil was going to try and finish me off this time. But you see, the Word of God is living and active. Sharper than any doubled edged sword, it penetrates even to the dividing of soul and spirit, joints and marrow. It judges the thoughts and attitudes of the heart according to Hebrews 4:12. In my heart, I knew that I loved the Lord Jesus Christ. I just had to find my way back to Him.

The Bible asks in the 8th chapter of Romans verse 35, *Who shall separate us from the love of Christ?* Shall trouble or hardship, the answer to that is no one or nothing can separate us from his love. It goes on to say in verse 37 that NO, *in all these things we are more than conquerors through him who loved us. For I am convinced that neither death nor life, neither angels nor DEMONS, nor anything else in all creation , will be able to separate us from the love of God that is in Christ Jesus our Lord.* I remember thinking and crying out to the Lord. I asked Him, "Lord, how did this happen to me Father?"

It was a slow, gradual transition. First, I stopped reading my Bible. Then, after a while I stopped praying. I allowed myself to get all wrapped up in work and started running around with people that I had no business getting involved with. The Bible says that bad company corrupts good character. Instead of being a good ambassador for the Lord, I fell. And the thing that is so amazing is that Christ still loved me. And loves us all, no matter what.

I was talking to a buddy of mine, today, that fell out of fellowship with the Lord as well. I told him that the hardest thing for me was the guilt. He said it was for him, too. He said that the thing that changed his thinking was when he read that back when Moses led the Israelites out of Egypt and the Lord had parted the Red Sea so they could cross over, that they made a golden idol and worshipped it. Even after the miracle that they had just seen the Lord do for them. And yet, He loved them and gave them another chance. I thought that was a great point. I can tell you that there is no peace like the peace you have serving Christ Jesus.

I called a dear friend of Mine in Baton Rouge. His Name is Keith Johnson and I told him everything. He immediately began to pray for me. The next few months were horrible. But Keith and his awesome wife, Kayla, kept praying for me. I couldn't call the ministers at Teen Challenge because of shame. But I knew if I could just drive myself to my knees, that I could get my head back on straight. It wasn't until a dear friend, that I hadn't seen in thirty years, came to Fort Worth to see me and I was exposed. Revette Richard caught me in the bathroom at my house smoking Crack. She was going through a divorce and drove all the way out there to see me. What she saw was a man who was very badly backslidden. She grabbed the Crack and flushed it down the toilet. I was battling so much guilt and shame. I knew that my mom and Greg would be so disappointed in me. I broke down and told Revette what I had done, that I had turned my back on the Lord. I told her about Teen Challenge and what I had been through.

She asked me where my bible was? I told her it was in one of my chest of drawers. She pulled it out and handed it to me. We stayed up until daylight praying and crying. She stayed at my house for a couple of days and helped me clean up the house. We read the Bible and prayed for three days. I called Keith and told him that I had hit my knees and was going to get back on track seeking the Lord again. Keith Johnson is a very dear brother that I love dearly, he and his wife. They are true servants of the Lord.

Revette has gone back to church and started seeking the Lord again. I hunt with Brother Greg and Brother Stanley and talk with Brother Stanley just about every week. I took my eyes off of the Lord for two years. It was so true what those men of God told me at Teen Challenge; that if I ever take my eyes off of the Lord, even for a second, I would be in a very scary place. I am so happy that I am back in the will of God. After I finally hit my knees and cried out to God, it was amazing at how fast God restored once again all the things in my life that were important to me. When we fall, we think that we are so far away from the hand of God when in fact, He is always right there with us, waiting on us and hoping that we will cry out to Him. The day will come when I will meet my Lord face to face and I'm sure that I will get to crawl up in His lap like a newborn child and He will wrap His loving arms around me and tell me that it's okay now. I am really looking forward to that day.

Leanne, once again, came back home and we decided we would both get back in church and serve the Lord. I am a blessed man for sure. I know my mother-n-law has probably wanted to kill me more than a couple of times. I'm really glad she is a Christian lady or I would be in serious trouble.

Leanne and I have joined an incredible church in Burleson, Texas. It's Turning Point Church. My Pastor's name is Jeff Wickwire. He is awesome. Our church is awesome. I am so blessed to have a pastor that preaches the truth and teaches the truth. That's right, these people love to worship the Lord every Sunday morning. We absolutely love our church. If you are ever in Fort Worth, come visit us at Turning Point. We are located right off of 35-W in Burleson.

One more note, I just want to say that we all have people that we draw strength from. I know what I went through and there is someone who I have the highest respect for, because I'm a nobody. Josh Hamilton has been down the same path that I went down. He was the major leagues MVP last year. He plays baseball for the Texas Rangers. One of the things I love most about Josh is that he gives the Lord Jesus Christ the glory first. I can't even imagine what kind of pressure that he is under. Yet, every time he gets awarded another accolade the first thing he does is give glory to the Lord Jesus Christ. Every minute of his life is under a microscope. I draw a lot of strength from him, knowing that someone of his fame has an awesome walk with the Lord. And so, please remember that Brother in your prayers.

As I was writing the last Chapter of this book, I got a phone call from Brother Stanley down in New Orleans at the Teen Challenge center. He was the bearer of some really heartbreaking news. He told me that Pastor David Wilkerson, the founder of Teen Challenge, had passed away. He had been in an automobile accident. His wife was in the wreck, as well, and was in critical condition. By his obedience to God, I was able to share with you my testimony on the saving grace of our Father in heaven. Pastor Wilkerson has been instrumental in literally thousands of guys, just like myself, being able to put down drugs and alcohol and come to have a relationship with Christ. My hope is that if any students Of Teen Challenge ever read this book, they will see how God is so faithful when it comes to blessing His children, but also how important it is when you graduate from Teen Challenge to do the simple things like daily reading your Bible and praying daily as well. Because it can all leave you if you don't stay locked in, with your eyes seeking His face.

The life I live now is a life of peace and happiness. The anger from within has been taken away from me by the Lord. He has replaced the anger with joy unspeakable. I hope you have enjoyed reading my first attempt at writing a book. God Bless!